THE
LOCAL HEROES
BOOK OF
BRITISH INGENUITY

D1413580

ADAM HART-DAVIS presents *Local Heroes*. A freelance writer and television presenter since 1994, he previously worked for YTV as a researcher and producer, devising both *Scientific Eye*, the most successful school science series on television, and *Mathematical Eye* (1989–92), as well as five programmes on Loch Ness for the Discovery Channel (1993). He is also a science photographer, and his photographs have appeared in a wide selection of publications. He has written seven books, including *Test your Psychic Powers* (Thorsons, 1995), *Thunder, Flash and Thomas Crapper* (Michael O'Mara, 1997) and *Science Tricks* (HarperCollins, 1997). He lives in Bristol, and travels by bicycle. . . .

PAUL BADER is the owner and managing director of *Screenhouse Productions Limited*, a television company which specializes in popular science programmes, and is producer and director of *Local Heroes*. He previously worked for YTV, producing medical, health and science programmes for the ITV network and for Channel 4. Among other programmes, he has worked on *Discovery, The Buckman Treatment, The Halley's Comet Show* and *On the Edge*. He lives in Leeds.

The
Local Heroes
Book of
British Ingenuity

Adam Hart-Davis
and Paul Bader

Sutton Publishing

First published in 1997 by
Sutton Publishing Limited · Phoenix Mill
Thrupp · Stroud · Gloucestershire · GL5 2BU

British Library Cataloguing in Publication Data
A catalogue record for this book is available from the British Library

ISBN 0-7509-1473-4

Cover illustrations, front (clockwise from top): Henson's aerial carriage; Edward Jenner (© Jenner Museum); John Napier (© Napier University); Adam Hart-Davis (© Paul Bader). Back: Adam Hart-Davis (© Paul Bader).

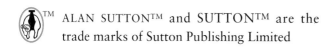 ALAN SUTTON™ and SUTTON™ are the
trade marks of Sutton Publishing Limited

Typeset in 10/14 pt Sabon.
Typesetting and origination by
Sutton Publishing Limited.
Printed in Great Britain by
Ebenezer Baylis, Worcester.

CONTENTS

ACKNOWLEDGEMENTS

The authors would like to thank the following individuals and organisations who generously provided illustrations for this book:

Saffron Walden Museum, p. 3; Jenner Museum, pp. 8, 9; Lincolnshire Library Service, p. 11; Dorset County Museum, p. 12; Mary Evans Picture Library, pp. 19, 21, 22, 56, 58, 82, 91, 92, 116/7; Emily Troscianko, p. 20; Russell Photo, p. 24; *Illustrated London News*, p. 25; Francis Trevithick, p. 29; Cyfarthfa Castle Museum, p. 30; Henry Bessemer's autobiography, p. 45; Avery, p. 59; Bude-Stratton Town Museum, p. 61; National Trust (Photo: Prof. R.L. Bishop), p. 63; the Royal Society, pp. 64, 74, 83, 84, 87, 101, 102, 103; Cavendish Laboratory, Cambridge, pp. 68, 69; Discovery Museum, Newcastle upon Tyne (Tyne & Wear Museums), p. 74; Yorkshire Museum, pp. 76, 77; Freshwater Biological Association, p. 79; Leslie Herbert Gustar, pp. 88, 89; British Geological Survey, p. 90; Whitby Literary and Philosophical Society, p. 92; Natural History Museum, pp. 95, 97, 98, 99; Philpot Museum, p. 100; York Minster Archives, p. 125.

The cartoons were supplied by Specs Art of Cheltenham; other pictures were provided by the authors.

INTRODUCTION

Local Heroes began on 7 August 1990 when Adam bought a mountain bike, deliberately choosing a fluorescent pink bike with yellow mudguards for maximum visibility – in order to stay alive. His plan was to get fit and thin by riding it to work two or three times a week, from Heckmondwike to Leeds, where he was a producer at Yorkshire Television. This was a round trip of about 25 miles, including three serious hills. The next day he reached the office gasping and dripping with sweat, propped the bike against his desk, and lay on the floor to recover. His boss suggested mildly that now he had a bike he could go and do something useful with it, like looking for local scientists.

Within a couple of weeks Adam was varying his routes, and while struggling up the long hill between Birstall and Drighlington he noticed a plaque on the wall of Fieldhead Farm, now perched above the M62, saying that it was the birthplace of a real hero of his, Joseph Priestley, the man who discovered oxygen. An hour's research revealed that Joseph's mother had died when he was nine, and he was sent off to live with his aunt; he had spent his teenage years at the Old Hall in Heckmondwike – which had become Adam's local pub, serving Sam Smith's beer and rather good lunches. Priestley's portrait is on the pub sign.

What's more, Priestley eventually moved to Leeds to be minister at Mill Hill Chapel, and lived in a house in Meadow Lane, right next door to the brewery, roughly where Tetley's brewery is now. Priestley was fascinated by the sight and smell of the heaving froth in the large open fermentation tanks called 'Yorkshire squares', and he discovered that by lowering a candle into the tank he could actually see where the fresh air ended and the 'fixed air' began – the carbon dioxide, as we would call it. The candle went out as he lowered it into the layer of carbon dioxide above the froth in the tank, and the smoke floated on top of the carbon dioxide, a foot above the liquid. This got him thinking about different types of air, and led to his discovery of oxygen – although he called it 'dephlogisticated air', which was hardly a catchy name, and Lavoisier got much of the credit.

Here then was an interesting story; a hero of chemistry born in a little old stone farmhouse, raised in what has become a pub, and discovering chemistry in a brewery – and all connected by a single bike ride. The idea of a programme was born.

Further research in the libraries revealed some extraordinary ingenuity in the Yorkshire area – the aeroplane, for example, was invented in Brompton by Sir George Cayley, and the idea of black

Adam Hart-Davis outside the Old Hall pub, Heckmondwike, West Yorkshire. On the pub sign is Joseph Priestley, the pioneer chemist, who lived at the Old Hall as a teenager. The pub was on Adam's cycle route to work, and inspired *Local Heroes*.

holes was dreamed up by the Rector of Thornhill, John Michell, who gave William Herschel a telescope. . . .

Adam so much enjoyed telling the stories that he was allowed to try doing so in front of the camera, and Paul was invited to produce the pilot programme. In due course Paul and Adam produced two regional series of *Local Heroes* for Yorkshire Television, but the exclusion of science programmes from the ITV channel was causing the YTV science office to shrink. Paul left to set up his own independent company and Adam left to become a freelance writer and photographer – and a presenter if possible.

Seven years have gone by and, amazingly, we are still working together, and are still fascinated by the tales of ancient ingenuity that seem to lurk in every byway. Experience has shown that the heroes who cause most delight on the screen are generally the people that no one has ever heard of. Everyone has some idea of what Isaac Newton did, but Winstanley, Moule, and Ayrton are hardly household names. And yet their stories are every bit as interesting as those of Newton and Brunel.

We have gradually developed a set of criteria for what makes good heroes for television. First, they have to be dead. We realised that if we started interviewing working scientists we could not tell rude tales about them; we should have to aim at some criterion of worthiness, and the whole character of the programme would be lost. What's more, much of modern science and technology is so intricate and complex that understanding what is going on and why it matters is difficult without a lot of experience in the particular field. On the other hand the ingenuity of the eighteenth and nineteenth centuries led to ideas and machines that were relatively simple and easy to understand.

We also like to pick on ideas or inventions that are easily illustrated. Thus William Hyde Wollaston's discovery of two new metallic elements was arguably his most important scientific achievement. However, his camera lucida, the device that allows duffers to draw, was a lovely invention, and much more appealing to people in general.

We began making the gadgets and putting on demonstrations almost as a way of helping ourselves to think through the ideas and the inventions, but when we put them on the screen people loved them, even though we are the first to admit we are not great carpenters or engineers. Now we deliberately keep them crude and unpolished, because they still serve the same function – they are there to illustrate ideas, not to demonstrate our DIY skills.

The Atmospheric Railway Inn, Starcross – scene of Brunel's spectacular failure.

In Georgian and Victorian days women were rarely educated; nor were they allowed to write or publish scientific papers, nor to join such institutions as the Royal Society. As a result, the number of local heroines is small. Such shining examples as Mary Anning and Florence Nightingale, however, show that where they could find a niche – and escape parental and peer pressure – women could easily hold their own with the men.

Once we have chosen a hero, we like to fasten on to one corner of the life and work. Isambard Kingdom Brunel was one of the most colourful of the Victorian engineers, and yet we chose to highlight one of his spectacular failures – the atmospheric railway in south Devon – not to make him look a fool, but because it was such a wonderful story, and because the technological idea was so clever and interesting. We never attempt to be comprehensive. Our aim is not to tell the whole story of Mr Brunel's life, nor to encompass every important engineer of Victorian times, nor even to expose every

hero from a particular place. Rather we want to illustrate the great range of British ingenuity with a variety of surprising stories. We even went to Chesterfield to tell the tale of railway king George Stephenson who retired there in the 1840s in order to grow straight cucumbers, thereby cleverly anticipating an EC regulation of 1993!

We are still amazed and delighted by these stories; we hope you enjoy them too. This book presents about sixty of the stories from the series, loosely grouped into areas of ingenuity. There's a chronology on pages 144–7 to help show how the heroes may have interacted, and a map on page 142 to show which locations are within your range, if you fancy a hero hunt!

Adam Hart-Davis & Paul Bader
March 1997

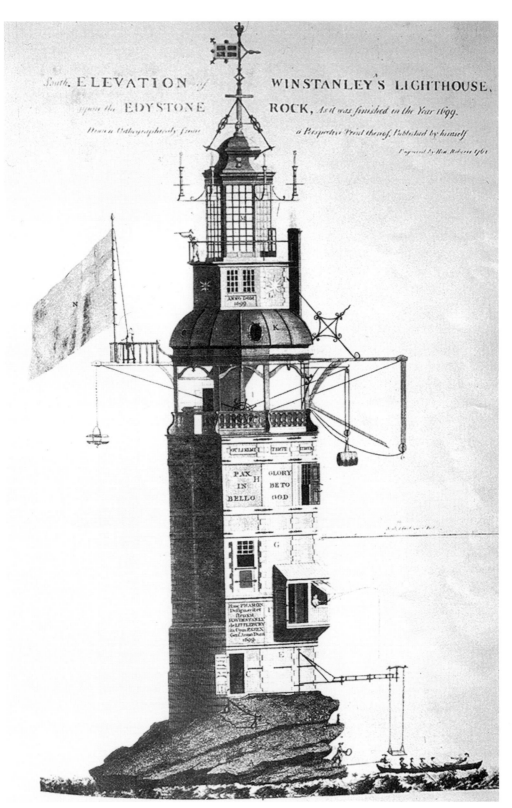

Henry Winstanley's engraving of his Eddystone lighthouse, complete with a lengthy caption describing the various rooms and extras, including the crane used to assist with landing materials in bad weather.

LIFE AND DEATH

Human beings are all too ready to make both friends and enemies. As a result, an enormous amount of ingenuity has been expended on ways to kill other people, and on ways to keep them alive – on medicine, and on weapons of war. The stories in this section are all concerned with life and death, although they present a rather sideways look at the business of mortality.

1. HENRY WINSTANLEY AND THE FIRST EDDYSTONE LIGHTHOUSE

Some 14 miles off Plymouth lies one of the most vicious reefs around the coast of Britain. The Eddystone Reef has been a sailors' nightmare for hundreds of years. Right in the middle of the approach to Plymouth, its hard red rocks just show above water at high tide, so they are difficult for a lookout to see, and present the most dangerous obstacle possible. Hundreds and hundreds of ships have been wrecked on Eddystone.

In 1688 William of Orange became William III. He brought his fleet of 400 ships into Plymouth for his first winter as king, and established his main naval

Henry Winstanley, engraver, joker, and self-appointed Gent.

arsenal there, in what is now Devonport. In 1694 he declared there should be a lighthouse on the reef. The only problem was, who could build it? This story is about the first Eddystone lighthouse, which was built at the very end of the seventeenth century by an eccentric joker and fabulous showman called Henry Winstanley.

Henry Winstanley was born at Saffron Walden in 1644, and became an engraver and builder of weird gadgets. He became rich, and bought five ships. Unfortunately, in 1695 two of them were lost on the Eddystone Reef. Winstanley rushed to Plymouth to investigate, demanded to know why there was no lighthouse on Eddystone, and when he heard they were looking for an architect he said, 'I'll build it!'

He had never built anything before – but then no one had ever built a lighthouse on a wave-swept rock in the open sea. There was only one possible site – the only rock big enough to put a lighthouse on. It was 30 feet across, it barely rose out of the waves at high tide, at a slope of 30°, it was harder than concrete, and it was 14 miles out to sea.

To get out there he had to set off from Plymouth with his workmen and their tools at high tide, so that the ebb helped them out of the Sound. Then by sailing and more often rowing for six hours they could with luck reach the reef just before low tide, and have two or three hours there before having to row back. Often the trip out took eight or ten hours, and more often than not the sea was so rough they could not even land, and simply had to go back again. To get there at all was possible only in the summer, between July and October, and even then the weather often prevented any trip for ten days at a time. The critics said it couldn't be done. . . .

The first thing to do was bore twelve holes in the rock into which he could fix heavy iron stanchions. Making those twelve holes took the whole of the first summer. In late October 1696 the twelve great irons were put in the holes and molten lead poured in round them to fix them firmly into the rock.

In 1697 they cemented stones to the rock around the irons, but unfortunately there was a war going on, and in June work was delayed when a French privateer turned up and captured Winstanley. The Admiralty sent a stiff complaint to the French, whereupon Louis XIV, realising that the French needed the lighthouse as much as the English, declared, 'We are at war with England, not with humanity!' He released Winstanley, tried to persuade him to stay

and work in Paris, and sent him back with loads of expensive presents. By the end of the second summer they had built a stone pillar 12 feet high.

On 14 November 1698 Henry Winstanley climbed up to the lantern and lit a dozen tallow candles. In Plymouth there was pandemonium. Fishermen came in with the astonishing news that Eddystone was showing a light; people flocked out on the Hoe with telescopes, trying to get a better view. Winstanley had done it! He had lit the Eddystone! The pubs were packed with sailors rejoicing and sometimes weeping – for the first time ever they would know where the reef was in the dark. The only people who could not join in the celebrations were Winstanley and his crew. The weather was so bad it was five weeks before they got back to land.

Winstanley's Tower was 24 feet in diameter and 120 feet high. His own

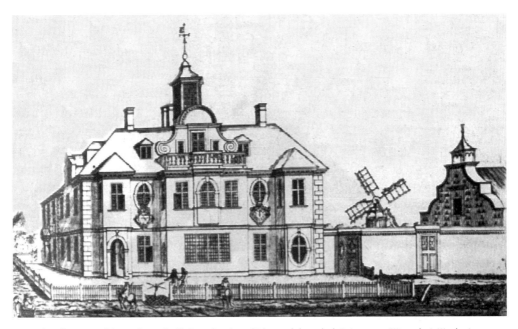

Winstanley's house at Littlebury in Essex. He filled it with tricks and jokes, and charged admission to see 'Winstanley's Wonders'.

engraving of the lighthouse was captioned to explain how it all worked: 'An engine crane that parts at joints to be taken off when not in use, the rest being fastened to the side of the house to save it in time of storms, and it is to be made use of to help landing on the rock, which without is very difficult.'

And up below the lantern: 'The State Room, being 10 square, 19 foot wide, and 12 foot high, very well carved and painted, with a chimney and two closets, and 2 sash windows with strong shutters to bar and bolt.

'The lanthorn that holds the lights is 8 foot square, 11 foot diameter, 15 foot high in the upright wall: having 8 great glass windows . . . and conveniency to burn 60 candles at a time besides a great hanging lamp.'

Above the entrance was a tablet that said (in Latin) 'H Winstanly of Littlebury in the County of Essex, Gent, designed and built this lighthouse, AD 1699.' (There isn't a Latin word for Gent, but he put it in anyway!)

For five years no ship was wrecked on Eddystone whereas before the lighthouse had been built one wreck a month was not uncommon. However, the weather was fierce and in the worst storms some waves broke right over the building. The keepers said the impact of the waves often knocked crockery off the table, and made them seasick. The critics said the lighthouse would never last – it couldn't survive the winter. Henry, fed up with the carping, boasted publicly that he had one crowning wish in life – to be in his lighthouse during the greatest storm that ever was.

His chance came in November 1703. There had been two weeks of severe gales, and all the ships coming in from the Atlantic arrived days early; meanwhile outgoing ships could not leave; so all the harbours and estuaries were crammed with ships. On Thursday 25 November came the lull everyone had been waiting for, and on Friday morning Henry went out to the lighthouse with his maintenance crew, to carry out repairs before the winter.

Just before midnight there blew up what may well have been the worst storm this country has ever seen. We know about it because the journalist and author Daniel Defoe toured round the country afterwards assessing the damage. Men and animals were lifted off their feet and carried for yards through the air. Lead roofs were ripped like tissue paper off a hundred churches. Fifteen thousand sheep were drowned in floods near Bristol. Four hundred windmills were blown over. A thousand country mansions had their chimney stacks blown down. Eight hundred houses were completely destroyed. And all those ships, crowded into anchorages, were blown into one another and on to the rocks; some eight thousand sailors were drowned that night, within yards of land.

Henry Winstanley's wish was mercilessly granted; he died in his lighthouse during the greatest storm that ever was. In the evening of Friday 26 November the Eddystone lighthouse showed a light as usual. By daybreak on Saturday there was no sign that the lighthouse had ever existed, except for a few bent pieces of rusty iron sprouting from the rock. . . .

Nothing remains of Winstanley's lighthouse, although the stump of Smeaton's 1759 lighthouse still stands on the same lump of rock.

2. HUMPHRY DAVY'S GASES FOR HEALTH AND LAUGHTER

As you drive into Bristol from the Cumberland Basin a magnificent city panorama unrolls. Dominating the left-hand side of the view is the Avon gorge, spanned high above the river by the delicate-looking Clifton Suspension Bridge, Isambard Kingdom Brunel's showpiece (although the money kept running out, and it was not finished until after he died).

Almost underneath the eastern end of the Clifton Suspension Bridge is St Vincent's Rock, from the bottom of which, during the seventeenth and eighteenth centuries, came gushing out warm murky water – 60 gallons a minute at 76 °F. This was Hotwells Spa. The water was believed to be medicinal, and people came here from far and wide to take the waters, including Catherine of Braganza in 1677. She set the trend for everyone who was anyone, and by the 1780s Hotwells was one of the most fashionable and most crowded watering places in the kingdom.

Many of the people who came to take the waters lodged along the road in Dowry Square, and so Dr Thomas Beddoes set up his brand new Pneumatic Institution at no. 6. This was funded by private subscription – they had £1,000 from potter Josiah Wedgwood, for example – and its aim was to find out whether the various gases that had just been discovered by Priestley, Lavoisier and others had any useful medicinal value. Dr Priestley, for example, said that breathing oxygen made him feel invigorated; would it perhaps be useful for patients who were ill, especially with diseases of the lungs?

The Institution could take eight in-patients and up to eighty out-patients. Many of them suffered from tuberculosis, which was a major killer, and all sorts of gases were tried in the attempt to find a cure. Beddoes apparently believed they might benefit from the gases produced by cows. It is unlikely that he actually took the cows into the ward, but he certainly kept a small herd in the garden next door, and piped the gases into the bedchambers. These gases, you understand, were what the cows breathed out, as well as what came from the other end . . .

If this had been effective, Beddoes would surely have been delighted, since the gases from the cows must have been produced at minimal expense! However, I imagine there was quite an incentive for the patients to say they were better and discharge themselves! Beddoes was the mastermind, but naturally he did not actually run the Institution; for that he hired a young Cornishman called Humphry Davy.

Humphry Davy was born in Penzance on 17 December 1778. He went on to run the Royal Institution in London; he was knighted, and became incredibly famous. But he was just nineteen when he came to Bristol in October 1798 as Medical Superintendent! The following year he heard about the new electric battery that had been invented by Volta in Italy. Volta said he made electricity just by holding dissimilar metals together. Davy was excited by this, but disagreed with Volta. He said you never got something for nothing; there must be a chemical reaction going on. He and Beddoes built a huge battery in the Pneumatic Institution in order to test out their ideas.

What's more, Davy argued that if chemistry could produce electricity then the same thing should work the other way round, and electricity should be able to produce chemistry. Thus he conceived the idea of electrochemistry, and later he went

Humphry Davy inhaled laughing gas from a green silk bag, while his patients were treated with the effluvia from cows.

on to use electrochemistry to isolate the new metals, potassium and sodium. The paper he wrote for the Royal Society about this was probably what got him invited to the Royal Institution in 1801.

But his real job in Bristol was to investigate gases. He made a variety, and tried them all out on himself. He almost died inhaling carbon monoxide, but he had a wonderful time when he found out how to make nitrous oxide, which came to be called laughing gas. The Department of Anaesthesia at the Bristol Royal Infirmary is named after Sir Humphry Davy, partly because nitrous oxide has become one of the most useful of all gases in medicine. When mixed with oxygen it is called 'gas and air', and it has a range of uses: it's used as a pain-killer in childbirth; it's carried by paramedics in ambulances; and it's used by dentists.

When you inhale it, as a 25 per cent mixture with air, the effect comes on within about four breaths, or 30 seconds. I found I felt tingling in my fingertips, which then went numb; I could jab them with a

pin without worrying. Nitrous oxide also reduces anxiety – which helps medical staff to give injections. There seems to be some argument about whether it really reduces pain or merely makes you not care about it. But perhaps that does not matter!

Being under the influence of nitrous oxide feels like being slightly drunk – having two large glasses of wine one after the other. Colours seem to get brighter – or the contrast increases. When you decide to move your head the view you see takes some time to catch up; there's a delayed response. Yet these effects disappear within a couple of minutes, and you can then drive a car safely! As long as you have oxygen as well you can take gas and air for hours. You will stay awake and lucid, although if the concentration is high enough, any joke may produce uncontrollable laughter.

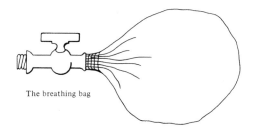

The breathing bag

Humphry Davy used to wander around Clifton breathing nitrous oxide from a green silk bag. He tried it out on all his literary friends, who loved it and danced in the streets. Samuel Taylor Coleridge said it made him feel as warm as when he came home to a fire after a walk in the snow. Southey wrote to his brother: 'O Tom! Such gas has Davy discovered . . . it made me laugh and tingle in every toe and fingertip. Davy has actually invented a new pleasure for which language has no name!'

The Pneumatic Institution was at 6 Dowry Square, an elegant private house in Hotwells, Bristol.

3. EDWARD JENNER AND THE FIRST VACCINATION

Finding out how diseases work and spread has always been difficult. Malaria was thought to be caught from bad air, which was why it was called by the name 'bad air' or malaria. Inventing useful treatments is even harder, and so I was surprised to find out that the killer disease smallpox was sorted out and dealt its death-blow before 1800, long before we had any effective plumbing or basic sanitation!

During the eighteenth century smallpox was a dreadful disease that almost everyone caught, and it killed one person in four; it was a worse killer then than cancer is today. It made millions blind, and those who didn't go blind got terrible scars on the face – the pockmarks from the pox. However, there was one group of people who never seemed to catch smallpox – milkmaids. These young women went around the farms milking the cows, and they were renowned for their prettiness; indeed it was enshrined in a popular song:

Where are you going to, my pretty maid?
I'm going a-milking, sir, she said.
What is your fortune, my pretty maid?
My face is my fortune, sir, she said.

One of the reasons they were so pretty is that their faces were not pockmarked, because they never seemed to catch smallpox. Most people thought this was just folklore, but some people took it seriously, and none more so than a young country doctor called Edward Jenner. He was born in Berkeley, in Gloucestershire, in 1749, studied medicine in London, and went back to be a doctor in his home town. For twelve years he was a medical journeyman – he had no permanent home, but rode about on his horse, staying either with his aunt or with any patient rich enough and willing to put him up for the night, and it was not until 1785 that he bought his own house, Chantry Cottage in Berkeley, for the princely sum of £600. It's now the Jenner Museum.

He was a scientist at heart, always asking questions. He was fascinated by hedgehogs, and measured their temperature when they were hibernating. He was also intrigued by cuckoos. He watched and described how the cuckoo chick pushed the rival chicks and eggs out of its nest. This work was so brilliant that

Edward Jenner, the dapper country doctor from Gloucestershire.

he was elected to the Royal Society, and was invited to go round the world with Captain Cook. He didn't go; perhaps he wouldn't have enjoyed three years at sea. He was a bit of a dandy; he rode about Gloucestershire on horseback, complete with shiny black boots and silver spurs, and he certainly noticed how pretty the milkmaids were.

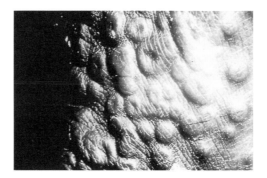

Cowpox sores on a cow's udder.

Jenner thought their apparent immunity was interesting, and started asking questions. The milkmaids told him that if they had caught cowpox, they would never get smallpox. Most people thought this was just an old wives' tale, but Jenner realized it might be a clue to saving the world from smallpox. Cowpox was a disease the cows sometimes caught; it produced nasty spots on their udders, and the milkmaids sometimes caught it, and got nasty sores on their hands. They usually felt ill for a day or two, but it wasn't serious. Jenner questioned milkmaids and doctors, and went on and on about his theory until he became a cowpox bore; so much so that he was banned from his local medical club.

People were so frightened of smallpox that many used to get themselves inoculated with it. That is, they were deliberately given smallpox. They knew they would get it only once, and they reckoned it was better to have it when they were fit and ready than if it came as a nasty surprise.

Jenner himself had been inoculated as a lad, and described the experience as really horrible. There were six weeks of preparation. He was bled to make sure his blood was fine; he was purged repeatedly until he became emaciated

and feeble; he was kept on a diet, small in quantity . . . and so it went on. Then he was taken to an inoculation stable and 'haltered up with others in a terrible state of disease' – the whole thing was a nightmare, although he didn't see anyone actually die during his inoculation. However, there was a significant chance of dying simply from this inoculation, and Jenner was determined to stamp out the practice. His idea was that if cowpox protected the milkmaids, perhaps he could inoculate other people with cowpox, and that would protect them too. He suggested this to his friends and colleagues, and met with incredulity and disbelief. He was ridiculed – people thought they might turn into cows – and many doctors said he was mad.

The only way he could think of to prove his theory was by testing it. One problem was that cowpox was rare; the Gloucestershire farms suffered cases only every few years. But in 1796 a cow called Blossom got cowpox, and the milkmaid Sarah Nelmes caught cowpox via a cut in her hand. On 14 May Jenner carried out his critical experiment.

He chose a healthy young boy called

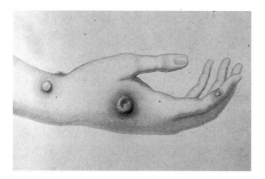

Cowpox sores on the hand of milkmaid Sarah Nelmes.

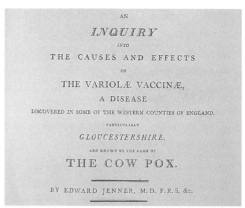

AN

INQUIRY

INTO

THE CAUSES AND EFFECTS

OF

THE VARIOLÆ VACCINÆ,

A DISEASE

DISCOVERED IN SOME OF THE WESTERN COUNTIES OF ENGLAND,

PARTICULARLY

GLOUCESTERSHIRE,

AND KNOWN BY THE NAME OF

THE COW POX.

BY EDWARD JENNER, M.D. F.R.S. &c.

Part of the title page from Edward Jenner's book on vaccination.

James Phipps, eight years old, who had never had either smallpox or cowpox. He summoned the lad and the milkmaid into his study in Chantry Cottage, and with his little penknife he made two small cuts or scratches, about half an inch long, on James's arm. Then he squeezed some pus from Sarah Nelmes's cowpox sores, and rubbed it into the scratches. Sure enough, James caught cowpox. On the seventh day he complained of a sore arm, and on the ninth he became a little chilly, lost his appetite, and had a slight headache. But on the day following he was perfectly well.

Seven weeks later, on 1 July, James Phipps was deliberately inoculated with smallpox – but did not catch it. He was inoculated with the dreaded disease again and again, but never caught it. Indeed he lived to a ripe old age. And the fact that he failed to catch smallpox was critical. Jenner had his proof.

Jenner had managed to untangle three interlocked notions – first that the milkmaids' immunity was real, second that immunity against one disease – smallpox – could come from a different disease – cowpox – and third that cowpox germs could be collected from people – in this case the milkmaid Sarah Nelmes. You did not have to wait for the cows to come home. The Latin word for cow is *vacca*, and Jenner's technique came to be called 'vaccination'.

Jenner had to wait two years for another outbreak of cowpox, so that he could do some more experiments, and he had to wait for ten years before people really took note of what he had done. Meanwhile he built a rustic 'Temple of Vaccinia' in his garden, where he vaccinated the poor for free.

In the end he won due acknowledgement for his achievement. In 1806 he was given £20,000, in recognition of what was described as 'the most important discovery in the whole history of medicine'. By 1812 more than a million people had been vaccinated, and in 1978 the last case of smallpox was recorded in Somalia. As a result of the observations and deductions of a simple country doctor, the killer disease smallpox has been wiped off the face of the earth.

Jenner's House, Chantry Cottage in Berkeley, Gloucestershire, is now the Jenner Museum; open during the summer; 01453 810631.

4. THE LONG DROP OF WILLIAM MARWOOD

Before 1875 a prisoner sentenced to death was hanged by being suspended on a rope and allowed to die slowly by strangulation. This barbaric procedure was changed by William Marwood, who worked out how to break the victim's neck, causing instant death.

Marwood was a Lincolnshire cobbler, with premises at 6 Church Street, Horncastle. Over several years he repeatedly applied for permission to act as hangman, and was finally given his first commission in 1875, when on 21 December he hanged Henry Wainwright in Lincoln gaol.

Marwood did not hide this part-time profession. He used to go to fairs and show off his ropes for sixpence a time. He put up a big sign above his shop, and he charged high prices for his bootlaces; people came from miles around and bought them because they were the hangman's laces. He became famous, and was frequently mentioned in music-hall songs and jokes, such as 'If pa killed ma, who'd kill pa?' Answer: 'Marwood.'

Before Marwood, death was slow and painful: the pressure of the rope crushed the windpipe, cutting off the supply of air to the lungs. A typical victim lost consciousness after three or four agonising minutes, and died after about ten. Marwood's idea was to use a long rope and a trap-door high up on a scaffold, so that when the trap was opened, the victim fell seven or eight feet before reaching the end of the rope. Marwood tied the rope snugly tight, with the knot at the point of the jaw under the victim's left ear. This ensured that when the rope tautened it snapped the head back, causing a fracture dislocation of the atlanto-axial junction. The top vertebra, the 'atlas', sits on the second one, the 'axis'. A peg of bone sticks up from the axis into a socket in the atlas, and allows the head to swivel. Put your fingers to the back of your neck, and you can feel the atlas turn with your head, while the axis below does not move. When the head is snapped back by the long drop, the peg breaks, the neck kinks rapidly, the spinal cord is crushed, and the resulting spinal shock causes instant loss of consciousness, even before the heart stops beating. Because it caused immediate brain death, Marwood's long drop was more humane that the previous method; he used to say of his predecessors, 'They hanged 'em; I execute 'em.'

Marwood's shop is marked by a plaque at 6 Church Lane, Horncastle, Lincolnshire; it is now part of the house next door.

William Marwood's strange little cobbler's shop in Church Street, Horncastle as it is today.

MARWOOD,
his Cobbler's Shop
and Trade Card.

WM. MARWOOD,

EXECUTIONER,

CHURCH LANE,

HORNCASTLE,

LINCOLNSHIRE, ENGLAND.

5. HENRY MOULE AND THE EARTH-CLOSET

In 1849 cholera struck Britain like a deadly tide, killing 55,000 people in a single year. Nowhere was worse hit than Dorchester, and in Fordington, just outside the city wall, the vicar worked tirelessly with the sick and the dying. On one day he held six funerals. They said Henry Moule stood between the living and the dead, boiling or burning contaminated clothes and bedclothes, and although he had not been popular, he gradually won the respect of the community. He also began to make the crucial connection between lack of sanitation and the spread of disease.

Moule described how, as he knelt beside a dying man, the overflow from the one privy shared by thirteen families trickled between his knees and the bed, and he saw the sewage bubbling up from the earth beneath the fireplace. Moule wrote to Prince Albert – the owner of the town – to explain the dreadful conditions; having written eight long letters without eliciting any sensible response, he set about his own methods of sanitary reform.

Henry Moule was born in Melksham on 27 January 1801, went to Cambridge, came to Fordington when he was twenty-eight, and stayed here for the rest of his life – more than fifty years. When he arrived with his wife Mary and two sons aged four and two, he found Fordington a sorry place. Thomas Hardy was to become a close friend of Moule's son Horace, and when he wrote *The Mayor of Casterbridge* Hardy used Mill Street, close by the vicarage, as the model for

Henry Moule, champion of the earth-closet, with his family and household at the vicarage where he did much of his research.

Mixen Lane – a slum of unmitigated horror, with gross overcrowding, appalling housing, poor sanitation and water; stinking ponds, crime, vice and prostitution.

Moule tackled his job with enthusiasm, making himself most unpopular with the parishioners by introducing a second fiery sermon in the Sunday service, and reforming the music until he drove the choir away. Moule even managed to get Dorchester races stopped. People jeered at his wife and children, and vandalised their lawn.

Undeterred, he ran the vicarage like a self-supporting commune, growing masses of vegetables, running a large hothouse, keeping cows, and earning some money by teaching not only his own eight children, but also seven paying boarders.

For some years he was chaplain to the troops in Dorchester Barracks, and he used the royalties from his 1845 book *Barrack Sermons* to build a church and also a school at West Fordington. He was an enterprising man; he took out patents for the steam heating of greenhouses and for a new kind of fuel for steam engines. This scientific attitude led him to a fascinating discovery.

In the summer of 1859 he decided that his cesspool was intolerably disgusting, not only to him but also to the neighbours. So he filled it in, and instructed his household to use a bucket instead. At first he buried the sewage in a trench in the garden, but he discovered by accident that in three or four weeks 'not a trace of this matter could be discovered'. In other words, the sewage had decomposed. He suspected dry earth was the active agent, and set about testing his theory. He put

up a shed, sifted the dry earth beneath it, and mixed the contents of the bucket with this dry earth every morning. 'The whole operation does not take a boy more than a quarter of an hour,' he wrote, '*and within ten minutes after its completion neither the eye nor nose can perceive anything offensive.*'

So the dry earth deodorised the sewage and produced rapid decomposition. Moule's next step was to bring the earth into the house, dry it in a metal box under the kitchen range, and mix it in the bucket after every use . . . And in due course he developed a brand-new earth-closet – a sort of commode, with a bucket underneath the seat. Behind the seat was a hopper which he filled with dry earth. When he had finished using the closet, he pulled a handle, and a measured amount of dry earth was delivered into the bucket, to cover the offering.

He found he could recycle the earth, using the same batch several times, and he began to grow lyrical with rage at water-closets and praise for the earth: 'Water is only a vehicle for removing it out of sight and off the premises. It neither absorbs nor effectively deodorises. The great agent is dried earth, both for absorption and for deodorising offensive matters.'

And, he said, he no longer threw away valuable manure, but got a 'luxuriant growth of vegetables in my garden'. He backed up this last point with a scientific experiment, persuading a farmer to fertilize one half of a field with earth used five times in his closet, and the other half of it with an equal weight of super-phosphate. Swedes were planted in both halves, and those nurtured with earth manure grew one third bigger than those

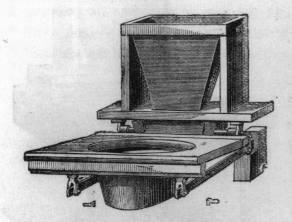

Apparatus No. V., " Self - acting," (*new patent*), is similar to No. III., except that it is sent out with an earthenware rim instead of with one of galvanised iron.

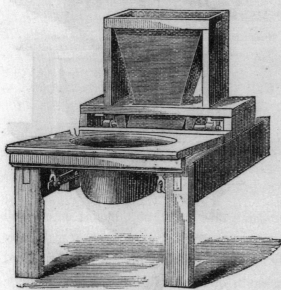

Apparatus No. Va., " Self - acting," (*new patent*), is similar to No. IIIa., except that it is fitted with an earthenware rim instead of with one of galvanised iron. The many advantages appertaining to apparatus No. Va. render it the most perfect form of self-acting dry closet apparatus yet produced.

NOTE.—*Apparatus Nos. II., IIa., III., IIIa., IV., IVa., V., and Va., are constructed under two patents, the first being by John Ward Girdlestone, A.D. 1870, 2nd September, No. 2398; and the second by John Ward Girdlestone, A.D., 1876, 3rd May, No. 1867.*

Apparatus No. IX., " Pull-up " (*new patent*). In this instance the user of the closet, previous to its use, sees nothing beneath the seat but an earthenware rim and a layer of clean dry earth, which last, resting on a valve beneath the rim, effectually conceals the contents of the receptacle. Here, on the handle in the seat being raised, after the

Page from an advertising pamphlet of the Moule Patent Earth-closet Company.

given only superphosphate. Moule quoted a biblical precedent for his efforts, from a set of instructions about cleanliness in Deuteronomy, chapter 23 verse 13: 'With your equipment you will have a trowel, and when you squat outside, you shall scrape a hole with it and then turn and cover your excrement.'

Many people think the earth-closet is a bit of a joke, but Moule was convinced that it was the future. He worked out the implications; if used by a family of six, the earth-closet would need 50 kg of earth per week; so a town of 10,000 would need 17 tons of earth a day – but only borrowed!

He took out a patent in 1860, and set up the Moule Patent Earth-Closet Company Ltd, which manufactured and sold a wide variety of earth-closets, the expensive models made of mahogany and oak. They were even manufactured abroad under licence – in Hartford, Connecticut, for example, by the Hartford Earth-Closet Company.

Moule wrote a string of tracts and pamphlets, including *The advantages of the dry earth system*, and *Manure for the million – a letter to the cottage gardeners of England*. He also tried hard to get government support, with an 1872 paper on *Town refuse – the remedy for local taxation*. His main point was that to provide mains water and sewers was fantastically expensive, and the sewage still had to decompose somewhere. If everyone looked after their own there would be enormous saving in taxation, and much less spread of disease.

He managed to convince a lot of people: 148 of his dry-earth closets were used by two thousand men at the Volunteer encampment at Wimbledon in 1868; 776 closets were used in Wakefield Prison. The combination of economy and health was powerful. In 1865 the Dorset County School at Dorchester changed from water-closets to earth-closets, eliminated smells and diarrhoea, and cut the annual maintenance costs from £3 to 50p! Lancaster Grammar School also brought in earth-closets, but for less scientific reasons: the water-closets were always out of order 'by reason of marbles, Latin grammar covers, and other properties being thrown down them'.

For some decades in the second half of the nineteenth century the earth-closet and the water-closet were in hot competition. Almost everything Moule said was true, and much the same arguments are used today by the champions of bioloos and composting lavatories. Unfortunately, flushing does rapidly remove the sewage from the house, and as a result – in rich countries – the water-closet is winning, for the moment. . . .

Henry and Mary Moule lie in the top corner of the graveyard below the church in High Street, Fordington, right outside Dorchester. Moule Close is beside the church. There is an original Moule earth-closet in Dorset County Museum; 01305 262735.

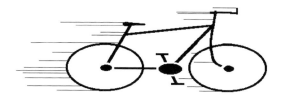

6. SANITATION AND STATISTICS: THE STORY OF FLORENCE NIGHTINGALE

The idea that cleanliness is next to godliness may have encouraged some members of the church-going fraternity to wash themselves, and medieval abbeys usually had lavatories – places to wash – but before about 1850 personal hygiene in this country was generally rare. Queen Elizabeth I astonished her courtiers by her enthusiasm for washing: she used to have a bath once a month, 'whether she needed it or not!'

Even though the Romans had organised extensive public baths in Bath and many other places, their example did not catch on. Until the middle of the nineteenth century there was little piped water in Britain; posh people washed their faces in bowls of warm water brought in by the servants; poor people used a stream or the village pond if they were desperate.

Cities without proper sewers were revolting, and people complained bitterly about the smell. In the hot summer of 1858, when the banks of the Thames were covered for miles with decomposing sewage, the 'Great Stink' was debated in Parliament, where the curtains had to be drawn and soaked in chloride of lime to allow the members to breathe.

However, most people failed to realise that lack of sewers and proper sanitation was a major cause of disease. In the mid-1800s, the infant mortality in English cities was 48 per cent; of all the babies born, only half lived to the age of five. They died from various illnesses – typhoid, cholera, diarrhoea – but basically they died because the sewage was not properly separated from the water supply.

The greatest advance ever made in human health was nothing to do with medicine, penicillin or surgery. It was the drive for simple sanitation, and it was brought about by such far-seeing doctors as William Budd and John Snow, and the remarkable Florence Nightingale, reluctant debutante and brilliant campaigner.

William Budd, having caught typhoid himself and recovered, took a deep interest when the disease struck his own village of North Tawton in Devon. By following its progress from house to house there and later in Bristol, he proved that it must be spread mainly in drinking water. John Snow came to the same conclusion about cholera in London's Soho, and took dramatic action – he removed the handle from the pump in Broad Street, where he knew the water was contaminated, and stopped the outbreak dead in its tracks.

Florence Nightingale's posh background made her an unlikely candidate for a heroine, but with her sharp insights, wide experience and missionary zeal, she revolutionised both the nursing profession and the management of hospitals. Her family travelled widely; she was born in Italy on 12 May 1820 in the city of Florence, and that's where she got her name. Her father was a wealthy bookish man, but her mother Frances cared only for society – where she was going to be seen, and with whom, what she was going to wear, which parties were beneath her station, and above all what were the marriage prospects for her two daughters.

Florence was supposed to behave like a lady, and occupy her time with flower-arranging and tapestry. She horrified her mother by going off and investigating hospitals, not just in England but even abroad, and she worked for three months at a hospital for the destitute – the Institute for Protestant Deaconesses at Kaiserwerth in Germany – where she was amazed to find many of the deaconesses were only peasants!

In 1854 the Crimean War broke out, and *The Times* sent out a reporter, William Howard Russell, who was in effect the first ever special war correspondent. He wrote back vivid reports about the bungling incompetence of the army commanders, and the horrors of the Crimea. In particular he wrote that although the French hospitals were well organised, the English wounded were terribly neglected. 'Are there no devoted women among us able and willing to go forth to minister to the sick and suffering soldiers?' he wrote.

Florence Nightingale answered the call. On 14 October she wrote to the Secretary of State for War, volunteering her services; on the same day he wrote to her, asking her to go. Their letters crossed in the post. Just one week later she set off, with thirty-eight nurses. In the hospital at Scutari, they found appalling suffering. There were no bowls for water. No soap, no towels. No mugs, knives, spoons. No proper food. There were four miles of beds, and the soldiers lay in them with wounds, cholera, typhus, frostbite – all jumbled together. They died in their hundreds – mainly of disease. A thousand men died of disease before the first battle began. Florence would not let men die alone and uncomforted, so she sat beside their beds as they died; in the next couple of years she personally watched some two thousand soldiers die.

She applied basic common-sense ideas of sanitation and proper food, and in due course the death rate came tumbling down. In February 1855, just after she arrived, more than 50 per cent of the men admitted to hospital had died. By June, the figure was down to 5 per cent.

When she came back from the Crimea she was summoned to see Queen Victoria at Balmoral, and she began her task of persuading people that reform was necessary. Her main weapon, rather surprisingly, was statistics. Statistics had become all the rage.

Florence had collected statistics on everything in her hospital, from admissions, discharges, and causes of death, to the number of drains and the distance between the beds. She presented her results in striking graphics that she called 'coxcombs'. The whole thing represents a year. Each segment is a month. The areas represent the number of deaths. The inner light parts represent deaths from wounds and the outer dark parts represent deaths from preventable disease. For every

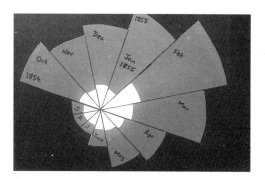

Florence Nightingale displayed her statistics in the form of 'coxcombs'. Each segment represents one month of the year. The areas of the coxcomb represent the numbers of soldiers who died in the Crimean war. The inner part represents the soldiers who died from their wounds; the outer part those who died of disease. For every soldier who died in battle, seven died from preventable disease.

Florence's modest face of the Nightingale family memorial at East
Wellow.

Florence Nightingale achieved two remarkable things. Before she came along, nursing was regarded as a menial job of drudgery; most nurses were illiterate women of loose virtue who liked their drink and had no concept of hygiene. She raised the status of nursing to that of a caring profession. She was hopelessly wrong in her theory of disease, but by a combination of common-sense, drive, plain speaking and sheer hard work, she managed to get through to the authorities and bring about massive reform in hospital management.

Yet when she was dying she refused burial in Westminster Abbey, and insisted on being buried without any special fuss in the family grave in East Wellow, near Romsey. On the big family memorial, where the other members of the family have their names carved in full, one on each face, her side simply says F.N.

Perhaps she would like to be remembered as the caring nurse. Remember those four miles of beds at Scutari? If she could not get round them all during the day, she carried on alone through the night, with her Turkish oil lantern – the woman they loved – the Lady with the Lamp.

*Florence Nightingale was buried in the tiny churchyard of
St Margaret's Church at East Wellow, near Romsey. The
Florence Nightingale Museum is in the corner of
St Thomas's Hospital in London; 0171 620 0374.*

soldier who died of wounds, seven died from preventable disease. In her report to the Royal Commission she wrote that every year the army took the fittest young men, and managed to kill 1,500 of them with poor food and disease. They might as well have been taken out on to Salisbury Plain and shot. These were ideas that people could understand.

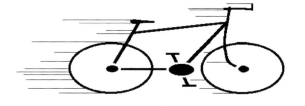

7. HEART DISEASE AND *DIGITALIS*: WILLIAM WITHERING, 'FLOWER OF PHYSIC'

The human heart is a tough little bundle of muscles, about the size of your fist, with astonishing powers of endurance and consistency. Its job is to pump blood around the body, and on every beat it squeezes the blood out with considerable force – enough to squirt perhaps 16 feet up in the air if you cut a major artery. The heart beats about once a second, 3,600 times every hour, thirty million times a year, for perhaps seventy years. That's more than two thousand million times, and the heart rarely misses a beat; it never has time off. So it's hardly surprising that in later life it sometimes goes a bit awry.

Two hundred years ago people died from cholera, typhoid and all sorts of other preventable diseases, and half of them died young, so that the average life expectancy was thirty or forty years. Today we have controlled those diseases, at least in the affluent parts of the world, and so people live much longer. This means that the heart is much more likely to run out of steam, which is why today heart disease is a major cause of death – not because our hearts are less healthy, but rather because we have removed many of the obstacles that used to shorten human lives.

One of the common forms of heart trouble is fast atrial fibrillation; the natural rhythm of the heartbeat breaks down and the heart races, feebly fluttering. The best-known treatment for this condition is Digoxin or Digitoxin pills, made from extract of the foxglove, *Digitalis purpurea*.

'The flower of physic', William Withering discovered the medicinal properties of the foxglove, *Digitalis purpurea*.

The meticulous country doctor who discovered *digitalis* was not a brilliant thrusting medical pioneer, but a tedious plodder called William Withering. Born at Wellington in Shropshire on 17 March 1741, he studied medicine at Edinburgh, and became a physician in Staffordshire, where his girlfriend persuaded him to take an interest in botany.

In 1775 two things happened that were to make his name. He found the foxglove, and he was invited to join the Lunar Society of Birmingham. This was a gathering of extraordinary scientific brilliance, founded in 1766 by tycoon Matthew Boulton, the vast and entertaining Erasmus Darwin (Charles's grandfather), and their doctor, William Small. The society met once a month, usually for dinner in Boulton's house, on the night of the full moon, so that they would have light to ride home again after dinner; that was why they called themselves the Lunaticks. When Small died, Darwin thought they should have another doctor, and introduced Withering, hoping that his 'philosophical taste' would appeal to Boulton, who promptly invited Withering to join the Society.

So Withering left his practice at Stafford, took over Small's practice, and moved to Birmingham. Meanwhile his girlfriend had interested him so much in plants that for years he had studied them, gathered and catalogued information, and in 1776 he published a huge botanical treatise with a ridiculously long title that started *A botanical Arrangement of all the Vegetables naturally growing in Great Britain. With descriptions of the Genera and Species According to the celebrated Linnaeus.* Erasmus Darwin tried to persuade him to change the title to something simple like 'British Plants', but he insisted on keeping the full twenty-four lines! They had quite a bitter argument over it, especially when Darwin discovered Withering was such a prude he had throughout the book avoided blatantly sexual words such as stamen and pistil!

Withering may have been irascible and a bit of a bore, but he was extremely successful. By the time he was forty-six he was the richest doctor in England outside London. He moved into Edgbaston Hall – an imposing building which is now Edgbaston Golf Club – and he had the distinction of having the first water-closet in Birmingham.

However, what made him really famous

was his interest in plants, and in particular in one gypsy remedy. One of his patients was dying of heart disease and Withering thought the case was hopeless. But the patient, unwilling to give up, took a gypsy remedy, and got better. So Withering spent months tracking down the gypsy in the savage outback of Shropshire to ask what this magic potion contained. The vital ingredient was foxglove.

The foxglove, *Digitalis purpurea*, remains an important source of heart medicine.

Withering was intrigued. He decided to do some experiments of his own, to find out whether foxgloves really were good heart medicine, and if so which was the best part of the plant. He tried every bit, in all sorts of different ways, and after experimenting on 163 patients found that the best formulation was dried powdered leaf, administered to the patients by mouth. This was in 1775 – and to this day there is no better treatment for fast atrial fibrillation than extract of the foxglove.

When he became very ill in 1799, his friends said, 'The flower of physic is indeed Withering.' And when he died a foxglove was carved on his memorial stone in the little church at Edgbaston.

William Withering lived in Edgbaston Hall, now Edgbaston Golf Club; his memorial in Edgbaston Old Church on Church Road has a foxglove carved in stone.

8. WILLIAM HARVEY'S BLOODY REVOLUTION

In medical science great advances are rare, but one of the most dramatic discoveries of the last five hundred years was how blood circulates round the body. In the early 1600s, the world expert on blood-flow was the great Fabricius de Aquapendente, at the University of Padua. Fabricius had invented the Anatomy Theatre, where even students in the seventh row were only 25 feet from the cadaver being demonstrated.

Although Padua University was a centre of revolutionary scientific thinking, the up-to-date authority on the circulation of the blood was Galen, a Graeco-Roman physician who had worked in the second century AD – some 1,400 years earlier. No new theory had emerged. Part of the problem was that proper

printing was only about a hundred years old, so ideas didn't travel quickly. It was also the done thing to celebrate classical authority, even though to a modern eye there was plenty of evidence to suggest that the doctrine of the ancients might sometimes be faulty.

There were two quite separate blood circulations, said Galen: the venous and the arterial. Venous blood was made in the liver and nourished the body. The blood constantly ebbed and flowed, being replenished by seeping through pores from the right to the left side of the heart. Generally, the blood moved out to the body during the day, and then was attracted back to the heart at night. The arterial circulation contained air from the lungs, which got rid of the heat from the heart, and was then breathed out.

Fabricius was interested in little lumps

William Harvey demonstrates the circulation of the blood to King Charles I.

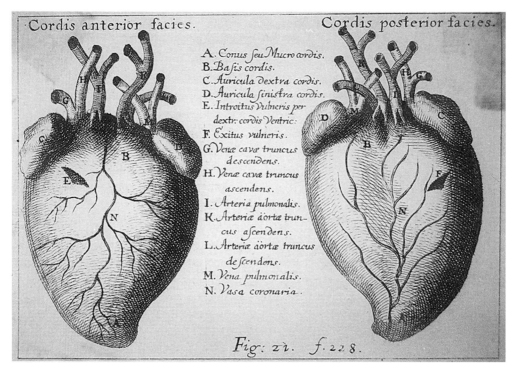

Harvey's brilliance in discovering the circulation of the blood is especially impressive because the techniques available in his day did not permit him to see the capillaries, which join the veins and arteries.

he could see in the veins; indeed he was credited with discovering them although in fact they had been known for some time. Since blood was supposed to be moving down the veins from the heart, what were these strange structures? He said their purpose was to restrict the flow and stop it reaching the extremities too quickly.

His students in the Anatomy Theatre included two young men – Galileo Galilei from Pisa and William Harvey from England. Galileo had done his experiments on falling bodies, but had not yet become famous over the moons of Jupiter. Harvey seems to have been born in Folkestone, Kent, in 1578, the twentieth year of the reign of Elizabeth I, probably on 1 April. His father was a merchant and had some inherited property, which made him wealthy enough

to send William to the best local school, the King's School in Canterbury. We don't really know much about William's boyhood, but he may have already fixed on a medical career when he left school, because he enrolled in Caius College, Cambridge, founded by Dr John Caius, a distinguished but rather old-fashioned anatomist.

In 1599 he suffered a nasty attack of 'quartian ague', what we call malaria, which was then a common disease in the marshy Fens. He must have made a pretty good recovery, however, because the next year, 1600, he went to Padua to study with Fabricius. Perhaps being a student with the brilliant and radical Galileo helped Harvey to think the unthinkable – that his teacher Fabricius might have entirely the wrong explanations for the valves in the veins, the function of the heart and the working of the circulation.

Harvey was a man of great brilliance, but also of great courage, because he had the nerve to say that 1,400 years of scientific thinking were wrong. He realised that the whole theory was nonsense. He experimented with veins from animals, and found that valves didn't just slow down blood flow from the heart; they completely stopped it. There was no way blood could flow down the veins; their only purpose, he said, was to take blood *towards* the heart. He also said that the arterial system was filled not with air, but with blood.

Anyone might argue with anatomical interpretations, but it's pretty difficult to refute simple arithmetic, which was Harvey's next weapon. He had dissected many living creatures, and realised that the heart was a pump, and that in humans it ejected 2 oz of blood every beat, 60 times a minute. So how much blood would Galen's venous circulation have had in it? With each beat the heart pumps 2 oz; so in a minute, it pumps 3.6 litres – about 6½ pints. Harvey worked out that in just half an hour 83 lb 4 oz of blood would be pumped out of the heart. The liver could not possibly generate all this blood, and anyhow there was no room for it in the body. His conclusion was clear: this was the same small amount of blood going round again and again.

Finally he worked it all out. The heart is a pump with two chambers. The left side sends blood to the body via the arteries. It comes back through the veins to the right side of the heart, which then pumps it round the lungs to get rid of carbon dioxide and take on more oxygen. The refreshed blood returns from the lungs to the left side of the heart, where the cycle begins again.

This was utterly different from the theory which had been accepted for 1,400 years, but after he published his book, as Harvey himself said, 'It will be very difficult for anyone to explain in any other way.' He began to explore these ideas in lectures from about 1616, and in 1628 finally published his great book, *Exertiato De Motu Cordis et Sanguinis in Animalibus: Anatomical Essay on the Motion of the Heart and Blood in Animals.*

Harvey lived almost to the age of eighty. He had a distinguished medical career, becoming chief physician at St Bartholomew's Hospital, physician extraordinary to James I and physician ordinary to Charles I. Although he was renowned in his own lifetime, we don't know much about his private life, although there is a famous letter from him revealing that his wife owned a talking parrot, and that he is reckoned to have been one of the first people to have become addicted to coffee!

Harvey was buried at Hempstead in Essex, not far from Saffron Walden, where there is not only a magnificent stone sarcophagus in the church but also forty-nine members of the Harvey family in the crypt below. The notorious highwayman Dick Turpin was baptised in the same church, and is reputed to have been born in the pub across the road.

William Harvey did much more than simply work out a few facts about the circulation. He was one of the first people to believe that argument and experiment were more important then ancient authority. He was a true founding father both of medical science and of modern scientific thinking.

Harvey was buried – above forty-nine other dead Harveys – in a fine marble sarcophagus in the church at Hempstead in Essex.

9. HERTHA AYRTON, AND THE END OF POISON GAS

In the early stages of the First World War, hundreds of thousands of soldiers were pinned in trenches by the machine-gun bullets whizzing overhead. To begin with, the commanders thought they could silence the machine-guns by bombardment with heavy artillery. They were wrong. On the first day of the battle of the Somme, when the troops went 'over the top' in the 'great push', struggling with the mud and the barbed wire, twenty thousand men died, probably within a couple of hours.

In the first six months of the battle, neither side advanced more than half a mile. The way forward eventually was

Mrs Ayrton in her Laboratory.

Before Hertha Ayrton, women scientists had to watch their husbands reading their scientific papers before the Royal Society.

found, in the shape of the tank, but meanwhile both sides looked for ways to kill the enemy where they were. They were dug down out of the reach of bullets, but they could still be reached by poison gas.

Thousands of artillery shells were filled with liquid gas; these exploded on impact and spread the gas. But probably more lethal were the cylinders stored in the front line. On suitable days, when the wind was blowing gently towards the enemy lines, the stopcocks were opened, and poison gas was allowed to roll silently across no-man's-land and into the enemy trenches, ravaging the unsuspecting troops. There was no warning – just a sudden curious smell, a choking sensation, and sometimes streaming eyes.

Many types of gas were tried. Chlorine, now used in very dilute form for disinfecting swimming pools, caused choking and lung damage. Mustard gas caused terrible irritation of the eyes; the soldiers could not see, and the skin often blistered. One of the most deadly was phosgene, with a sweet smell of new-mown hay, but lethal after-effects.

Troops were issued with gas-masks, but wearing them all the time was impossible; what was needed was a way to get the gas out of the trenches when it had drifted in. The solution was the Ayrton Fan.

Phoebe Sarah Marks was born on 28 April 1854, one of eight children of Alice and Levi Marks, a clockmaker. Later, in her teens, she changed her name to Hertha. Fascinated by science, she went to Cambridge and on to Finsbury Technical College, where she assisted Professor William Ayrton in his research with arc lamps. She did well; not only did she work out what made arc lamps so noisy; she also

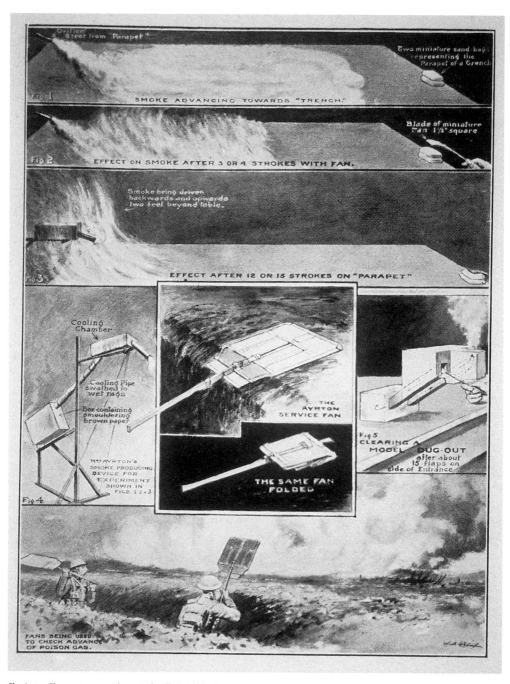

The Ayrton Flapper in use, as shown in the *Illustrated London News*.

married the Professor in 1885, becoming Hertha Ayrton. In 1899 she became the first woman member of the Institute of Electrical Engineers, as a result of her arc-lamp work. In 1902 she was proposed for election to the Royal Society, but was rejected because they had no legal charter to elect a married woman as a Fellow. Her breakthrough came in 1901, when she spent the autumn in Margate. The wide curving beach below the town is a lovely place to walk, and at low tide presents a fascinating array of ripples in the sand. To her sharp scientific mind they presented a challenging question – how and why were ripples formed?

One afternoon Hertha shocked her landlady when she returned from her walk and declared, 'I will have my bath in the sitting room after tea, please.' Hertha used the galvanised tub to perform the first of many experiments on sand ripples. She had already realised, from her observations on the shore, that ripples are not formed by waves crashing on the beach. So presumably they can be formed in deep water by the back and forth movement of the water above. If you look closely at the sand near a small bump, you can see that the water swirls over it and eddies back toward the bump. This swirl, or vortex, carries sand with it, makes the bump a bit bigger, and starts to make a trough where it took the sand from. When the water flows back the other way, the same thing happens on the other side of the bump. As the water ebbs and flows, each vortex takes more sand from the trough and dumps it on the bump. So the bump becomes a ripple. Back in London Hertha started serious research on ripples, which was to last for many years. In 1904 she became the first woman to read a paper to the Royal Society; needless to say it was about the origin and growth of ripples.

In 1915 the troops in the trenches in northern France were dying in huge numbers from the effects of poison gas. Like everyone else in Britain, Hertha Ayrton was worrying about them when she went to the Royal Society on 6 May. On her way home in a taxi – she lived at 41 Norfolk Square, near Paddington – she had a brainwave. If a flow of water can create vortices, then the opposite should also be true: the right type of vortex should be able to create a flow of air, which could drive back the gas.

She walked into her house and told her maid she was not to be disturbed for the rest of the day. Then she set about testing her idea by means of a table-top experiment. She built a small-scale parapet with little sand bags, and flapped a postcard on her 'sandbags' to create a local vortex, hoping it would generate a flow of air along the table. Then she made some smoke to monitor the flow of air. If a postcard could drive away the oncoming smoke, then perhaps a full-size fan would be able to drive poison gas out of a trench. Her results were so astonishing that she 'laughed aloud at the simplicity of the solution'. It turned out to be so effective that a close friend of Hertha's, Mr Greenslade, used to demonstrate its use in training trenches in 1916 using cyanide gas – without a gas-mask! As a direct result of her scientific curiosity and intuition, the Ayrton Fan was developed, and 104,000 were sent to the trenches to save the soldiers from the lethal drifting gas.

There is an original Ayrton Fan at the Imperial War Museum. She lived at 41 Norfolk Square, near Paddington station.

TRAINS AND BOATS AND PLANES

Walking, running and swimming may get people from place to place, but they can be frustratingly slow, and when there are loads to be carried, people are not the best pack-animals. Horses provide more power and more speed, but that merely whets the appetite. People have always wanted more rapid means of transport, partly so that they can get there before anyone else, and partly for the sheer exhilaration. Above all, watching birds soaring overhead makes the adventurous yearn to fly.

10. RICHARD TREVITHICK AND THE FIRST STEAM LOCOMOTIVE

The history of steam engines and trains is frequently confused. Most people think that James Watt invented the steam engine and George Stephenson the railway, but they are wrong on both counts. The first working steam engine was patented in the year that James Watt's father was born, and the first steam locomotive ran in 1804, ten years before Stephenson built one. The world's first steam locomotive was actually built by a Cornishman, Richard Trevithick.

Richard Trevithick was born on 13 April 1771 in Illogan, near Camborne in Cornwall. After doing hopelessly badly at school, he got a job as an engineer at a mine, and his life gradually unfolded as a catalogue of disasters: he was a giant in the field of engineering, yet not one of his inventions brought him wealth. He was swindled, and declared bankrupt; he almost drowned in South America, and he died penniless. Fierce yet tender-hearted, buoyant yet easily depressed, brilliantly ingenious and recklessly imprudent, Trevithick was the most Promethean of inventors.

He had the most amazing strength. One of his tricks as a young man was to carry about a blacksmith's half-ton mandrel. Another favourite was to write his name on a beam with his arm fully extended – and a 56 lb weight suspended from his thumb. He once joined in a sledge-hammer-throwing contest in which the aim was to hit the wall on the engine-house opposite. No one else could get it near; Trevithick hurled the hammer clean over the engine-house roof. And in one wrestling match, he turned his burly six-foot challenger upside-down and stamped the imprint of his boots in the ceiling!

Cornwall was an ideal place for a young engineer. The Cornish mines had been worked since Roman times, so to get to the remaining ore, miners had to tunnel deeper – but the deeper they tunnelled, the more water they struck. This water had to be pumped out, using either Newcomen steam engines or the improved machines built by Boulton & Watt of Birmingham. The Cornish didn't take kindly to this 'foreign' invasion, and they repeatedly tried to improve Newcomen's engine, so as to rival Watt's; but the terms of Watt's patent were so wide that the Cornishmen were constantly accused of infringing it. However, James Watt's patent expired in 1800, when Trevithick was twenty-nine.

He had realised that not only could the engine be made more powerful by using high-pressure steam to move the piston, but that he could do away with the condenser, and by replacing the cumbersome beam with a simple rod, he could make it portable. Soon his engines were replacing Boulton & Watt engines in the Cornish mines. But that was only the start. Now that Trevithick had built a portable engine, he could in principle use mechanical traction in place of horses. He built a model that he demonstrated on his kitchen table in 1799, and he had a full-scale steam carriage – the 'Puffing Devil' – ready on Christmas Eve 1801. On 28 December he set off on a 3 mile test run. Unfortunately, after about a mile, he hit a water gully. The overturned carriage was soon righted, but across the road Trevithick spied a pub. He went in for a drink to celebrate the first mile, then he had another . . . and another. They were still celebrating when the engine boiled dry and the road carriage exploded.

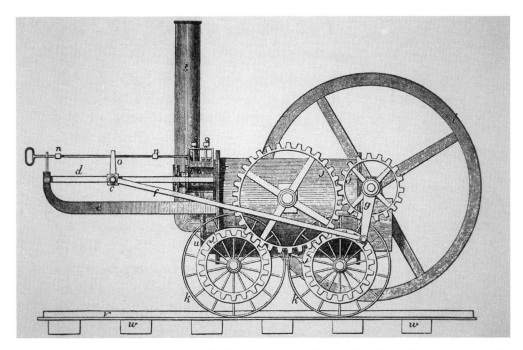

Trevithick's Penydaren Locomotive, the first in the world. Although he was twenty-five years ahead of George Stephenson and the *Rocket*, Trevithick missed out on the railway boom and died a poor man.

Not a man to be easily discouraged, Trevithick took out a patent for the high-pressure steam-engine, and in 1803 went to Merthyr Tydfil to sell some of his engines to Samuel Homfray, master of Penydaren Ironworks, where pig iron was made and transported down the valley to Cardiff. While he was in the Taff valley, Trevithick watched the horses pulling the wagons laden with pig iron along the iron railway to the canal, and he reckoned that his engines could do the job instead. Homfray backed the idea. In fact, he was so convinced it would work that he wagered another of the mine captains, Anthony Hill, 500 guineas that Trevithick's locomotive would haul 10 tons of iron from the Penydaren works to Abercynon Wharf and pull the empties back, by steam power.

Now Trevithick had to make his dream work, and the day of the great trial was set for 21 February 1804. Trevithick's locomotive was hitched to five wagons, carrying 10 tons of pig iron and 70 passengers, including Anthony Hill. They had some problems: one was that the chimney was too tall to pass under overhanging branches; so they had to cut down a few trees on the way. But they made it; the locomotive hauled its load the full 9¾ miles of track – in a speedy four hours and five minutes, making an average of a little over 2 mph. It was the first train journey in the world! You can still see the remains of the track where the journey took place, along the old tramway that is now the Taff Trail cycle track. The grooves in the stones where the rails used to lie are clearly visible.

The reason that Hill was so confident in waging 500 guineas and declaring the

Merthyr Tydfil ironworks.

journey impossible was that, like everyone else, he believed you could not get enough friction between the wheels and the rails to pull the load of a train. Trevithick's solution to this was weight; he built his engine up to 5 tons, which meant he had plenty of traction on the rails, especially as he had to haul the load downhill to Abercynon.

However, the track had been built for horses rather than 5-ton engines, and many of the cast-iron tramplates were broken by the massive beast, and Trevithick had to drive it back on the road. As a result the wager was declared void and, more importantly, Trevithick's locomotive didn't catch on. Homfray and other mine owners were not prepared to replace their tram tracks with stronger – and more expensive – ones capable of carrying steam locomotives. This did not become economically acceptable until the cost of horse fodder mounted during the Napoleonic wars a few years later. By then, Trevithick was in South America seeking his fortune, but some young engineers in the north were happy to make

locomotives for the new tracks – Matthew Murray and George Stephenson.

Trevithick made another engine to run on a circular track in London; he called it 'Catch me who can', and charged an admission fee of 1 s. He issued a challenge to run his engine for twenty-four hours against a racehorse. But no one took up the challenge, and he closed the show, having not even covered the cost of laying out the railway.

He went off to Peru, and spent eleven years making and losing fortunes in mining. By the end, he was surviving by eating monkeys and wild fruits. He just avoided being eaten by an alligator in Colombia, he almost drowned, and he ran out of money. By an amazing chance, he met in a hotel a young man who paid for his passage home – George's son Robert Stephenson. Trevithick got home in 1827, and died penniless six years later.

The Penydaren locomotive ran down to Abercynon on what is now the Taff Trail, south of Merthyr Tydfil; a replica locomotive at the Welsh Industrial and Maritime Museum in Cardiff runs on the first Saturday of each summer month. Open 10–5; 01222 481919.

11. ISAMBARD KINGDOM BRUNEL AND HIS ATMOSPHERIC RAILWAY

In 1844 there was railway mania. All over the country companies were being set up and permanent way laid down. The Stephensons and Locke had started in the north-west, while the Great Western Railway had been built with speed and enthusiasm by a young, thrusting, dynamic engineer; even his name was over the top: Isambard Kingdom Brunel.

Son of French engineer Marc Isambard Brunel and Sophia Kingdom, Isambard was born on 9 April 1806. As chief engineer for the Great Western Railway, he built Paddington station and Bristol Temple Meads, and invented Swindon. He designed the Clifton Suspension Bridge, the Tamar Bridge, and many others. He also built some of the first great iron ships – the *Great Western*, the *Great Britain*, and the gigantic *Great Eastern*, which in 1866 laid the first cable across the Atlantic.

For Isambard Kingdom Brunel, only the biggest and best was good enough. His projects were usually years late and

hopelessly over budget, but he was the showman of the engineers. Even his top hat was vast, and he used to carry his plans in it. Once, when he was introduced to Queen Victoria, he bowed low, swept off his hat . . . and his plans cascaded across the ground.

The railway reached Bristol in 1841 and Exeter in 1844, and Brunel became engineer to the South Devon Railway, incorporated on 4 July 1844 with a capital of £1,100,000. He chose a flamboyant route down the west bank of the Exe, and along the seashore to Dawlish and Teignmouth, where the trains still thunder along within yards of the sea. And he persuaded the directors of the SDR to approve the latest and most fashionable propulsion system. It had been tried out on a couple of test lines, but this was to be the first major railway designed from the start to be atmospheric.

The rails were normal, but on the sleepers between them was a cast-iron tube, 15 inches in diameter. A close-fitting piston ran along inside the tube, and was connected to the leading passenger car. The air was pumped out of the tube in front of the train, thus creating a vacuum; so the piston was pushed along by the pressure of the atmosphere behind it, and the piston pulled the train. It was indeed an atmospheric railway.

The piston was connected to the train by a rod which passed through a 3-inch wide slot along the top of the cast-iron tube. The slot was closed by a continuous flap of leather strengthened with iron framing and hinged along one edge, the other edge closing on the opposite side of the slot, the whole being made airtight with grease. The leather flap lifted to allow the rod to pass, and was then pressed shut again by a roller behind.

The vacuum was created by huge Boulton & Watt steam engines driving air pumps in pump-

A section of cast-iron tube from the atmospheric railway. The arm connecting the train to the piston ran in the slot at the top of the tube, which was sealed by a leather flap in the flanges on either side.

houses every three miles along the track. This created tremendous force. Suppose they pumped half the air out of the tube, and lowered the pressure inside to 8 lb/sq. in, then the force acting on the piston would have been more than half a ton – more than enough to move a lightweight train. On one epic test run outside Dublin, a young man called Frank Ebrington got into the front carriage, didn't realise the other carriages had not been coupled to it, and was hauled along a sharply curving track at a terrifying average speed of 84 mph. For the 1840s he was certainly the fastest man on Earth!

After many teething problems the South Devon atmospheric railway was opened to the public in September 1847. By January 1848 atmospheric trains were running all the way from Exeter to Newton Abbot. When the train reached a station they telegraphed ahead to the next pump-house and told them to switch on the pumps and make a vacuum ahead of the train. When all the passengers were aboard, the brakes were released and the train slid silently forward.

The passengers loved it. The trains ran quietly and smoothly, and without steam, smoke or smuts. What's more, they were often on time or even ahead. Speeds of 40 or 50 mph were normal, and one train ran from Newton Abbot to Exeter in 20 minutes, which is faster than today's Intercity trains! Because the trains didn't need locomotives they were much lighter, and so had tremendous acceleration and deceleration. Also the rails could be lighter and cheaper.

The SDR atmospheric system cost £300,000 to install, and worked more or less satisfactorily for nine months, but then it ran into all sorts of problems. Casting the pipe was difficult; eventually it was done in Bristol by Tom Guppy, brother-in-law of Sarah Guppy (see p. 128), who managed to turn it out at the rate of a mile a week. Even more of a problem was the leather flap along the top. It had to be there to maintain the vacuum, but in the winter it sometimes froze solid and let in the air, while in the summer it dried out and cracked. In an effort to solve the problem and maintain the vacuum, greasers walked along the track smearing the leather flap with a mixture of lime soap and seal oil, or whale oil. Unfortunately the oil attracted rats, and the rats ate the leather – and that didn't do the vacuum any good either.

There were also pumping problems. When they switched on in the morning each pumping station was like the inside of a vacuum-cleaner bag; the first rush of air brought a mixture of oily water, rust, and dead rats and mice. The telegraph never worked, and the leather seal leaked; so the pumps had to run continuously to maintain the vacuum. This was very expensive. There were other technical hitches. Atmospheric trains could not reverse; if they over-ran the platforms by a few yards, the passengers had to jump out and push the train back in. Shunting around stations was impossible. What is more, no one solved the problem of points – one track could not meet another, because there was no way of getting the rolling stock across the cast-iron tube between the rails.

However, what finally scuppered Brunel's atmospheric railway was a piece of financial sharp practice. In 1844 railway fever had been at its height, and Brunel had persuaded the Board to go atmospheric with a flurry of magnetic personality and the promise of cheaper running. By 1848 the tide had turned. The atmospheric system was out of fashion, and by a bit of dubious accounting the anti-atmospheric lobby managed to persuade the shareholders that the railway had made a loss in the first six months of the year. This was unheard of; no railway company had *ever* made a loss. In fact, they were owed a great deal of money for carrying mail, and the company was moving sharply into substantial profit, but the fudged accounts were enough; the atmospheric system was voted out. The last atmospheric train went up the line in the early hours of Sunday 10 September 1848, and the system closed down for ever.

When Isambard Kingdom Brunel worked himself to death at the age of fifty-three, his long-term friend and assistant Daniel Gooch wrote in his diary that he was a 'man with the greatest originality of thought and power of execution, bold in his plans but right. The commercial world thought him extravagant, but although he was so, great things are not done by those who sit and count the cost of every thought and act.'

The only remaining pumping station is next to the Courtenay Arms at Starcross, on the A379 5 miles south of Exeter; it now houses the Starcross Fishing and Cruising Club. A section of the cast-iron tube is displayed in the GWR Museum at Swindon; 01793 493189.

12. JUST THE TICKET! THOMAS EDMONDSON

Some inventions look so obvious with the benefit of hindsight that it seems extraordinary that they took so long to appear. A good example is the printed railway ticket. Railways began to provide serious transport in the early 1830s, and to start with every ticket was written out on paper by hand and every passenger's name written down in a big book in the booking office. This was a laborious business, and for any complex journey distributing the money was a nightmare, since there were more than fifty different railway companies.

The breakthrough came in 1837 at Brampton, 12 miles east of Carlisle, where the railway station was built a mile and a half out of town so that it would not interfere with the horse trade. The man with the vision was the station-master, Thomas Edmondson.

Edmondson was born in Lancaster on 30 June 1792. He was always fiddling with things, and when he was a small boy his mother, seeing that he could never be kept out of mischief, taught him to knit so that he would at least be quiet and useful. Later he connected the baby's cradle to the butter churn, so that when anyone was making butter they rocked the baby at the same time. He became a cabinet-maker and went into business in Carlisle, but it failed, and he became bankrupt.

So at the age of forty-four he joined the Newcastle & Carlisle Railway and became station-master at Brampton – and had to suffer all the inefficiency of manual ticketing. One day, walking across a field, he had a vision: the process could be mechanised. Tickets could be printed for

Edmondson was ticket-clerk at Brampton when he had the idea for his ticket system.

particular journeys, numbered, dated, and finally clipped when they'd been used. The whole system apparently came to him in one single flash of inspiration.

Unfortunately the Newcastle & Carlisle Railway said there would be no demand. Luckily for Edmondson – and us – in 1839 the brand new Manchester & Leeds

An Edmondson-style railway ticket, numbered by his special machine.

Railway offered to double his salary if he would go and work for them and introduce his system. Within a few years it was in use not only throughout Britain but all over the world. And his system was so effective and so simple that it wasn't bettered for 150 years – until computers came along.

He did well from his invention, by patenting it and charging a royalty of 10s per mile per annum – in other words any railway company using his system paid him 10s a year for every mile of track; so if they had 30 miles of track they paid him £15 a year. And according to the history books 'he worked out his invention with skill and patience, enjoyed its honours with modesty, and dispensed its fruits with generosity'.

Trains still stop at Brampton Station, 12 miles east of Carlisle, although it now has neither buildings nor a station-master.

13. TIME, TIDE, AND MUD: TED WRIGHT AND THE FERRIBY BOATS

The black muddy banks of the Humber at North Ferriby, just upstream from the Humber Bridge, are bleak and featureless – hardly a promising place for a great discovery. Yet thanks to the persistence and skill of a local teenager, Ferriby turned out to be the site of one of the greatest archaeological discoveries of modern times, which in turn revealed the quite unexpected engineering skills of Bronze Age Yorkshiremen.

In the 1930s young Ted Wright and his younger brother Willie were already keen on geology and fossil-hunting. They made regular trips to the Ferriby deposits, just a mile from their home, to look for molluscs, insects and animal bones. Naturally they hoped to find tools and other human artefacts, but without much success. However, they kept returning to the site, with its layers of flint, peat and clay, because the repeated washing by the waters of the Humber scoured away layers of mud, leaving more solid things sticking above the surface.

The tides in the Humber reveal some parts of the bank only every few years. In early September 1937 conditions were good, and the boys were busy probing with walking sticks and scraping with their trowels at anything that looked promising. Suddenly Ted came across three massive objects projecting from the mud at a shallow angle. Although only nineteen, Ted was expert enough to realise that these were the ends of huge planks of wood, and he thought he knew what they were part of. He called to his brother that

Ted Wright posing on the muddy banks of the Humber at North Ferriby, holding a model of the Ferriby Boat he discovered as a teenager.

he had 'found a Viking ship'. Willie was naturally sceptical, but wandered over to take a look. 'By God,' he said, 'I think you have.'

A little more scraping revealed what an extraordinary find this was. Beneath the mud they found that the planks were still connected, stitched together with what turned out to be twisted yew. The joints were packed with moss and the edges of the planks seemed to have a sort of tongue-and-groove arrangement. The boys had never seen anything like it. Just as astounding was the size of the boat. Prodding with their walking sticks, they found as they walked that for about 20 feet the remains went deeper below the surface, and then for a further 20 feet

The shaped planks were held together with yew stitches. On the underside of the boat the stitches were cleverly concealed within the planks to prevent chafing when the boat went aground.

became less deep. They unearthed the other end of the planks nearly 43 feet away. They were soon forced by the rising tide to abandon the boat.

Ted went up to Oxford, but managed to return to excavate the boat further in 1938 and 1939, helped by members of Hull Geological Society. A trench dug across the boat revealed that it had five bottom planks, together with the remains of one side plank. The stitching fascinated them: the yew 'withies' were tied through holes in the planks, and then over long pieces of wood which ran the length of the seam. These sealed the seams and held in the moss packing. They still had no idea how old the boat was, and they tried to find parallel discoveries. There were none.

The investigation was now cut short by the outbreak of war, which took Ted away from the Humber, apart from infrequent military leave. On one visit home, when the bank was particularly 'clean', Ted went down to see if more of the boat had been revealed. There was a bit more detail, but the really amazing discovery came 160 feet away from the original site. Clearly visible was the end of the centre plank of a second boat – Ferriby 2.

It now became clear that the scouring action of the tide which had revealed the boats in the first place, now threatened to destroy the remains, which were soft and couldn't stand unsupported. They back-filled the digs as much as possible, but had to cut off a couple of yards length of Ferriby 1, which would otherwise have been destroyed. Ted removed more in 1943. Some timbers were stored at the Wrights' home in North Ferriby, the rest were deposited with Hull Museum for safe keeping. Sadly they were destroyed when the museum was bombed.

Nothing more could be done until 1946, when a full-scale rescue of the now dangerously exposed boats was organised; it was almost a disaster. The director of the National Maritime Museum at Greenwich was keen to salvage the boats intact. This was going to be difficult because the site was exposed for only four hours between tides. The plan was to dig trenches down both sides of the first boat (F1), leaving it stranded on a clay plinth. A steel plate would then be dragged underneath it, slicing off the boat in a block of mud, which could then be dragged up the beach using the steel plate as a sledge. But as the plate slid under the boat, the mud began to move, breaking the fragile timbers. They were forced to slow down – but the tide was rising. Having exposed so much of the boat, the rescuers faced seeing it destroyed in the strong Humber currents. Ted then took what he described as one of the hardest decisions of his life: taking a saw, he cut his beloved boat in two. When it was done, he put his head down and wept while the exposed half was dragged up the beach to safety.

Ted wasn't to see the boats again for twenty-five years. The timbers were taken to Greenwich for conservation, and he embarked on a career in industry. He never stopped thinking about the boats, trying to work out how they had been made – and when. He thought they must be very old, but most authorities would not put them before 'early medieval', because they were so sophisticated. In 1951 radiocarbon dating was invented, but the one British laboratory equipped to carry out this process had a massive waiting list. The eventual result was staggering: the boats were 3,300 years old: Bronze Age!

So how were these boats used? There were no signs of rowlocks, and Ted concluded the boats had been paddled, a view confirmed by the discovery of a paddle of the right age. Taking the Humber's fierce currents into account, he calculated that eighteen paddlers would be needed to power a boat during the mile-and-a-half crossing – which neatly coincides with the likely number of seats. Before the Humber Bridge was built, Ferriby was an important crossing place, and the Ferriby Boats were probably used to transport passengers and goods, including cattle – some of the stitches show signs of having been kicked by hooves.

The boat timbers met with a sorry end. The primitive conservation process did not work, and the tanks containing the boats became smelly. Although the order to destroy the boats was not carried out, they were allowed to dry out, so these spectacular treasures from the Bronze Age are not suitable for public display.

This would have been the end of the story, except that in 1963 Ted was once again on the mud at Ferriby, this time with his son,

when he spotted something. 'Stand still, Rod,' he ordered, 'and don't move until I tell you. You are standing on the third boat.'

There's a reconstruction of a Ferriby boat in the Greenwich Maritime Museum, and the mud near the north end of the Humber Bridge is still thick and dark and pregnant with secrets. Plaques in the riverside car park at North Ferriby tell the story.

14. WILLIAM COPPIN AND THE GREAT NORTHERN

For thousands of years boats have been built of wood, and although one or two were made of iron in the eighteenth century, large iron ships were not built until the 1840s. One of the most famous was Brunel's *Great Britain*, but the first of the large iron ships was the *Great Northern*, built in Northern Ireland by Captain William Coppin.

William Coppin was born in County Cork on 9 October 1805, twelve days before the Battle of Trafalgar, and the sea was in his blood. At the age of fifteen he rescued six customs men when their boat capsized in the River Shannon, and when he finished school his parents sent him off to Canada to learn about boat-building.

He came back to Ireland and built a 100-ton ship – the *Kathleen* – when he was only twenty-four. Then he was commissioned to build a 600-tonner, the *Edward Reid*. He delivered it himself to a timber merchant in Londonderry. He loved the place so much that a few years later he went back to live there.

Coppin was a good sailor, and captained a number of other ships in the next eight years, including paddle-steamers to Philadelphia and passenger ships to Liverpool, before buying a boatyard on the River Foyle below the soaring battlements of Londonderry. There he built many ships, of every size and

Captain William Coppin (1805–95).

kind. The most spectacular, and the most famous, was the *Great Northern*, which was launched on 23 July 1842. At 220 feet long, and with a displacement of 1,750 tons, she was the biggest ship ever built in Ireland. She was rigged as a 50-gun frigate. She had three masts, and carried a full set of square-rigged sails, and a huge 370 horse-power steam engine which drove an Archimedes screw propeller, 12 feet in diameter, thundering round at a stately 88 rpm. The launch was such an event that twenty thousand spectators gathered to watch, crammed on every bit of dock, on the rooftops, and on sixty boats offshore. Even the Donegal Grand Jury insisted on coming, and the court was closed for the day!

Coppin sailed her round to London, because he hoped to sell her to the British Government. Unfortunately this was the only voyage the *Great Northern* made, for after a long and expensive delay, while Coppin sat in dock biting his nails, the British Government said 'No thanks;' perhaps they thought it would be unwise to buy a warship from Ireland. Coppin, now almost bankrupt, had to sell the ship for scrap to pay the harbour dues.

In his later life Coppin turned to salvage. Lots of ships sank, and in deep water they were extremely hard to reach. But they often had on board not only valuable cargo, but expensive steam engines, well worth recovering. So William Coppin thought hard about how to get down to the wrecks and bring them up. In 1876 he patented an amazing new diving suit. It was revolutionary in two ways: when you dive down more than a few feet in the sea, you are subjected to great pressure – go down to 30 feet and you have double the pressure at the surface, at 60 feet, three times the pressure, and so on. Coppin's new diving suit had two waterproof rubber skins, separated by tough ribs that would withstand some of this extra pressure, and so make life easier for the diver. It was the first attempt at a partially armoured suit. He also invented a better system for breathing out. Before then, divers had had to exhale straight into the water, which meant they had to breathe out against all that pressure. Coppin's new suit brought the used air back to the surface, so he could control the pressure at which they breathed out. With his brilliant new equipment, Coppin claimed he could go down to 120 feet and stay there for an hour – which was a great advance on what had been possible before.

He developed a cunning technique – to plug all the holes in a boat with clay, and then fill the hull with air, so that it floated to the surface. Coppin had realised that bubbles of air under water have immense lifting power. Archimedes' Principle says that the uplift is equal to the weight of water displaced. So if you fill a large ship with air, when it's under water, the uplift should be almost a ton for every cubic metre – more than enough to float the ship to the surface!

Coppin was a prolific inventor. In 1886 he patented an electric fish-catching apparatus – which looks like a winner, if you can believe the picture on the box!

However, the strangest Coppin tale is not about the captain, but concerns his young daughter Louisa, known to the family as 'Weesy'. She was born in 1846, and died on 27 May 1849, aged only three and a half. Six months later a ball of bluish light appeared in one room of the house. Curiously, the other children weren't frightened; they said it was just Weesy, come back to visit them. They used to chat to Weesy's ghost, and ask it questions. One day they asked what had happened to Sir John Franklin, the great explorer, who had gone off past Newfoundland to look for the north-west passage to India. He had set sail two years earlier with the ships *Erebus* and *Terror*, and no trace of the expedition had been seen since. The blue ball of light apparently produced a map on the wall, which showed the whereabouts of the ships and the expedition. Coppin noted the details and in May 1850 went to see Lady Franklin, who was so convinced that she launched another expedition to search for them in the spot identified by Weesy's ghost.

William Coppin's grave is in St Augustine's churchyard, high up near the battlements of Londonderry. His home down the hill at Ivy House – 34 Strand Road – has become a pizza restaurant.

William Coppin's *Great Northern* made only a single voyage.

15. EDWARD LYON BERTHON AND HIS FOLDING LIFEBOATS

In April 1912, on her maiden voyage, the 'unsinkable' SS *Titanic* hit an iceberg and sank. Because there were not enough lifeboats, 1,490 people drowned in the icy waters of the north Atlantic. Had she been equipped with Berthon folding lifeboats, most of those people might well have survived.

Edward Lyon Berthon was born in 1813. He did rather badly in school, and often had to write out lines as punishment; so he tied three quills together to speed things up a little. This triple quill was one of the earliest examples of his inventive genius.

After training as a doctor he entered the clergy, and eventually went to Romsey in Hampshire, where he was rector of the abbey for thirty years. Like most men of the cloth, he spent a lot of time repairing the church. Unlike most vicars, Berthon used boat-building techniques because he was obsessed with everything nautical.

A friend of his nearly drowned when his ship sank, and there weren't enough lifeboats for all the passengers. Berthon decided this was intolerable, and devised an amazing folding lifeboat. It was made of lengthways timbers, joined by waterproof fabric and pivoted at the ends; so the boat folded like two Japanese fans, joined at the tips. Three or four of these boats fitted in the space of one ordinary lifeboat; they occupied little space on the deck of a ship. They came in various sizes, from little ones designed for six to huge beasts that could carry over a hundred people. The design was simple and clever. There was one layer of canvas outside the wooden ribs, and another layer inside. When the boat was hung in davits over the side of the ship, it unfolded automatically, under its own weight. Then the bottom boards and thwarts were pushed in, and held the ribs and sides of the boat apart; so it was locked into its final shape. The two layers of canvas then formed a series of air-filled buoyancy tanks between the ribs, so that the boats would not sink even if they capsized.

Berthon had great difficulty getting his lifeboat accepted. He tried every dodge he could think of to bring it to the attention of the authorities. One day he took the prototype to sail on the Serpentine in London, hoping to get it noticed there. As luck would have it, Queen Victoria had finally got to hear of his fabulous folding lifeboat, and demanded a demonstration. Unfortunately she wanted to see it at eleven the next morning – at her house on the Isle of Wight. By the time he received the royal command it was already four o'clock in the afternoon. Berthon immediately hired three Hansom cabs and used the horses to tow the boat to the railway station, put it on the train and eventually made his royal date with fifteen minutes to spare. The Queen

The Revd Edward Lyon Berthon.

Small collapsible life-boat with carrying cart.

28 FT. BOAT WITH 75 MEN IN HER.   ABBEY CHURCH OF ROMSEY IN THE BACKGROUND.

Berthon used to test his life-boats in the river at the back of Romsey Abbey, where he was rector.

The SS *Orion*, whose failure to provide lifeboats for all on board inspired Berthon to design a collapsible lifeboat.

was impressed and instructed the Admiralty to test the boat.

Perversely, the Admiralty tested the lifeboat not by 'rescuing' sailors, but by firing a 21 lb mortar from it; the lifeboat sank, killing a midshipman. The Admiralty reported that it was 'useless'. However, all was not lost, since twenty years later Berthon lifeboats became standard equipment on troop-carrying ships. The Berthon Boat Company built hundreds of folding lifeboats, one of which is shown on a stained glass window in Romsey Abbey. The chap in the middle is Edward Berthon, and on the other side of him is another of his inventions – a type of telescope.

On 28 June 1834 Berthon was sketching on a ferry on Lake Geneva. When a splash of water from the paddle-wheel landed on his sketch-book, he pondered on the inefficiency of paddle-wheels. He reasoned that the whole thing should be under water, so it couldn't splash and would waste less energy. When he returned to Britain the following year, he set

about solving the problem. His first idea was to use a spiral like the screw thread on a bolt, only bigger. He thought he would need several turns of thread to get a good grip of the water. But his experiments suggested otherwise. He dug a huge ring-shaped pond in his garden, and sailed a model boat around it using different sorts of screw, and timing each version. Every time he shortened the screw, the boat went faster, until he ended up with not ten turns, not five, not even one, but one-sixth of a turn. The rest of the screw, it turned out, was simply slowing the boat down through friction. Berthon called his invention the 'screw propeller'.

Surprise, surprise, the Admiralty mocked the idea, stating that it 'was a pretty toy which never would and never could propel a ship'. Berthon was so dispirited by the Admiralty's response that he gave up. A few years later another man, Francis Smith, had the same idea and after many years of argument he managed to get the screw propeller accepted. Eventually, the two men had the satisfaction of watching a naval review in which three hundred Admiralty ships were all powered by screw propellers. Nowadays, of course, screw propellers are standard.

Another of Berthon's inventions he called the Nautochrometer, or Perpetual Log, and this one did amuse the Queen. The old method for measuring speed was to tie a piece of rope, knotted at measured intervals, to a lump of wood – the ship's log – and throw it off the back of the ship. The log dragged the rope out, and by counting the knots in the rope as they went past you could calculate your speed – in knots.

Berthon wanted to produce a device which showed the ship's speed continuously. His invention was essentially just a piece of pipe. The closed end of it stuck down into the water, and had a hole drilled in the side. As the boat moved along, the water rushing past this hole lowered the pressure just inside, by the Bernoulli effect. At the top of the tube was a manometer – water or oil in a U-tube. When the boat was stationary, the level of the liquid would be the same in the two arms of the U, but when it was moving, the reduction of pressure would make the liquid lower in one arm than the other. The faster the boat moved, the greater the difference in level; so you could read off the ship's speed directly in knots from the level of liquid in the tube. Berthon fitted one of these indicators to Queen Victoria's yacht *Victoria and Albert*. Apparently she used to spend hours watching the liquid levels going up and down in the U-tube, and liked to think that hers was the fastest ship in the world.

A stained glass window in Romsey Abbey shows Edward Lyon Berthon with one of his folding lifeboats, and his head is carved on one of the choirstalls.

16. HENRY BESSEMER'S ANTI-SEASICKNESS BOAT

Seasickness can be a nightmare; many people start to feel queasy long before the mooring ropes are cast off, and spend even the smoothest Channel crossing retching miserably over the rail. One such person was Henry Bessemer, millionaire and steel king, and he decided to do something about it. He didn't just take pills; he designed and built the SS *Bessemer* as a permanent preventer of seasickness.

Henry Bessemer was born near Hitchin, Hertfordshire, on 19 January 1813. His father was a rich engineer, and Henry

Henry Bessemer (1813–98).

always enjoyed messing about with scientific and technical things. When he was seventeen, and in love, he made his first serious invention – embossed stamps to use on title deeds. People who needed a £5 stamp would usually peel one off an old deed, and thus avoid buying a new one. The government was losing £100,000 a year in revenue. His invention made this impossible, and he convinced the Stamp Office at Somerset House. They offered him the post of Superintendent of Stamps, at a salary of £700 a year – a small fortune in 1830! He was over the moon – now he could marry his beloved.

She then had an even better idea, which was simply to print a date on the stamps. When he told the Stamp Office, they said, 'Thanks very much, brilliant; we won't need you as Superintendent of Stamps now.' And he got nothing at all for his invention.

This made him furious; two brilliant ideas, but no money. After that, he found out about patenting. In all he took out 150 patents, covering a huge variety of ideas.

His first fortune came from making brass powder to use in 'gold' paint. His sister had made a portfolio of her paintings of flowers, and asked him to do the title on the outside:

STUDIES OF FLOWERS
FROM NATURE
BY
MISS BESSEMER

He thought this deserved better than just ink; so he went to a shop and bought some 'bronze powder' in two different colours, and had to pay 7s an ounce for it. He realised that if he could make this stuff cheaply he could also make a fortune. So he invented machines to do it. The first one failed, but the second was a success.

Reckoning that a patent would not protect this process; he determined to keep it utterly secret. He had the full-size machines made in sections all over the country, and assembled them himself in his house in St Pancras, north London. He hired his three brothers-in-law to run the plant, and kept every room locked and the whole factory sealed against snoopers. Only five people ever went into the building, and they managed to keep the process secret for thirty-five years – much longer than a patent would have lasted.

But he really became an international jet-setter when he invented the artillery shell. The army were still using cannon balls, but Henry was sure that if they used a long thin projectile it would be not only heavier but also more accurate, because you could cut spiral grooves around it which would make it spin, and keep it on target. He built his own mortar, and made some experimental shells, which were highly successful. So he took out a patent in November 1854, and then tried to sell his idea to the War Department. They weren't interested; but a few months later he happened to have dinner with Napoleon in Paris. He sold the idea of shells to Napoleon, and had several trips to Paris on expenses. Unfortunately he found he was a terrible sailor; every time he crossed the English Channel he got horribly seasick.

The trouble with his new heavy shell was that the existing gun barrels weren't strong enough to take the extra pressure; so he decided to find a way of making better steel – which was how he came to invent the Bessemer Converter, which made him several million pounds.

Henry Bessemer was an astonishingly successful inventor and businessman; he was knighted in 1879. But I am relieved to say that even he did not always get it right. His most dramatic failure was the Bessemer Saloon Ship Company. He had suffered terribly from seasickness on his trips to France; so in December 1869 he began to spend time and a lot of money designing and making a cross-Channel boat in which no one could be seasick. He had two ideas. First, the boat was to be very long and thin, so that it would have minimal pitch – the ends of the boat would not go up and down much. Second, the entire cabin was mounted in gimbals with a great weight or even a gyroscope underneath it, so that however rough the sea was the cabin would always stay horizontal; while the hull of the boat would just roll and pitch about it.

He built a little model of his boat, but people remained unconvinced; so he constructed a full-sized mock-up of the cabin in a mobile hut mounted on a huge deck in a field near his house. He used a large steam engine to make the deck rock and roll, and then tried to keep the cabin horizontal. People still said it would never

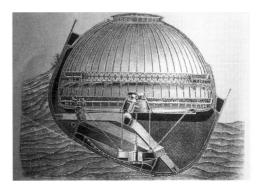

The SS *Bessemer* was designed to prevent seasickness, because the cabin remained upright when the ship rolled.

work, but he went ahead anyway, and spent more than £40,000 on floating the company and the boat.

Unfortunately, the huge heavy moving cabin made the boat so unstable that she was impossible to steer. On her maiden voyage on 8 May 1875, a beautiful calm day, the ship sailed from Dover, and in broad daylight comprehensively demolished the pier at Calais. The SS *Bessemer* never sailed again, and the company sank without trace!

Henry Bessemer ran his steel works from Bessemer House, which still stands on Carlisle Street in Sheffield. The last Bessemer Converter to run stands outside Kelham Island Industrial Museum in Sheffield.

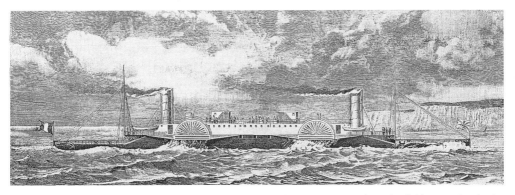

Bessemer clearly hoped the stable saloon of the SS *Bessemer* would enable passengers to travel in unheard-of luxury; in fact the ship proved impossible to steer and demolished the pier at Calais.

17. THE 'VERY NEARLY SUCCESSFUL' SUBMARINE OF GEORGE WILLIAM GARRETT

We were both intrigued and sympathetic when we first heard about a steam-powered submarine that was 'very nearly successful'. It was designed and built by an Irish vicar, George William Garrett.

Garrett was born in Dublin and went to Trinity College. He became a curate in Moss Side, Manchester, and later an honorary commander in the Turkish Navy – Pasha Garrett. But what endears him to us is that in 1878 he established the Garrett Submarine, Navigation, and Pneumatophore Company, and in 1879 he designed and built the world's first mechanical submarine – powered by steam. She was 45 feet long and carried a crew of three. The boiler was stoked while she was on the surface, and then the fires were damped down and she submerged, using diving rudders. In theory she could stay under water for four hours, and do 10 miles at two or three knots, using latent heat to supply power. Garrett had a dream that hundreds of his submarines would form a defensive ring around the British coastline.

The Navy recognized her potential, especially in view of the impending hostilities against the Russians. They offered Garrett £60,000 if the submarine passed marine trials in Portsmouth. So he organised a parish fête to raise funds, built his submarine, and launched her from Birkenhead. Unfortunately the weather was seriously bad and she ran into a storm off Rhyl in North Wales. The crew were taken off by lifeboat, and the submarine sank. She was called *Resurgam*, which is Latin for 'I will rise again' – but unfortunately she never did.

However, at Christmas 1995 divers found the submarine lying about 50 feet down on the seabed, with the hull intact and apparently in good condition. She has been declared a Maritime Treasure; so perhaps one day she will live up to her name.

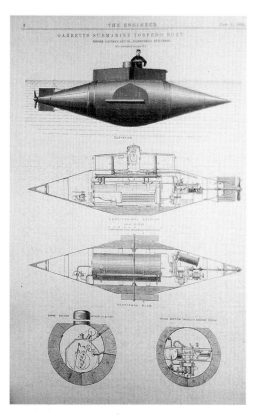

The *Resurgam* was described as 'very nearly successful' – not quite good enough for a submarine.

Resurgam *lies in 50 feet of water off North Wales.*

18. THE FIRST POWERED FLIGHT, BY JOHN STRINGFELLOW

People have always wanted to fly. The ancients imagined gods and angels soaring through the heavens, and created such legends as that of Daedalus and Icarus, who made wings from feathers stuck on with wax. In the eighteenth century hot-air balloonists took to the skies, but not until the middle of the nineteenth century were successful flights made by machines that were heavier than air.

Most people think the aeroplane was invented by Orville and Wilbur Wright. In fact, the world's first powered flight took place not in America in 1903, but at Chard in Somerset fifty-five years earlier, and the man who made it happen was John Stringfellow.

John Stringfellow was born in Attercliffe, on the outskirts of Sheffield, on 6 December 1799. When he was a teenager his family moved to Nottingham, and he went into the lace industry, becoming a bobbin and carriage maker – which meant essentially a precision engineer. The lace trade suffered badly from the Luddite riots, and some lace-makers decided to move to the calmer county of Somerset. John Stringfellow became the leading bobbin and carriage maker in Chard.

In 1827 he married American Hannah Keetch; they settled in Combe Street and had ten children, number four being John – always known as Fred – who wrote the only eyewitness account of his father's work.

John Stringfellow lectured on electricity to the Chard Institution, and in 1831 he launched a hot-air balloon to celebrate the coronation of William IV. He developed amazing skill at making steam engines. In about 1842 he teamed up with William Samuel Henson, an aeronautics enthusiast, and they began to discuss how to fly. They worried about what shape the wings of a plane should be, and how light it would have to be. They reckoned it would be sensible to use birds as models, so they took a muzzle-loading duck gun and shot all kinds of birds, which they weighed and measured, trying to find some mathematical connection between weight and wing dimensions. Eventually they settled on the rook: 'Henson and me generally took the rook as our standard as carrying half a pound to a foot. This bird can be seen any day leisurely flying at a speed not more than 20 miles an hour, and we considered that if we kept our machine within these limits we had a fair chance of success.'

Their basic idea was this. Take any wing – a bit like a bird's – keep it at an

John Stringfellow.

Replica of John Stringfellow's steam-powered aircraft in the Chard Mill where he achieved the first powered flight.

angle and push it through the air, and it will generate lift. Stringfellow once shot a square of cardboard across the room, saying, 'Any surface will hold the air with applied power.' This is interesting; most people didn't believe you could apply power to a surface and make it fly. They thought the wings of an aircraft would have to flap, like a bird's.

Stringfellow used to go up to London to visit Henson, and used the train journey to do experiments with the lift generated by various surfaces; he leant out of the window and gauged the lift of wings held in the airstream.

Henson was tremendously ambitious. In 1842 he not only applied for a patent for a 'Locomotive Apparatus for Air, Land, and Water' but also tried to set up an airline! The patent drawings show a monoplane with a 150 foot span, fabric-covered wings, an enclosed cabin, and tricycle undercarriage. Much of the detail – such as the bracing system – is quite original, but the details suggest that the drawing is in fact for a much smaller craft. The craft as specified would not have been strong enough, would not have met the weight criteria, and would have been under-powered. He was granted his patent, for 'certain improvements in locomotive apparatus and machinery for conveying letters, goods and passengers from place to place through the air,' but the proposal for the Aerial Transit Company had to go to Parliament, where it was greeted with derision.

Henson made a model of the plane in his patent; it weighed 14 pounds and had 40 sq. feet of wings. He tried to fly it in the Adelaide Gallery in London, but it was a complete flop – literally. The press had a field day; the papers were full of

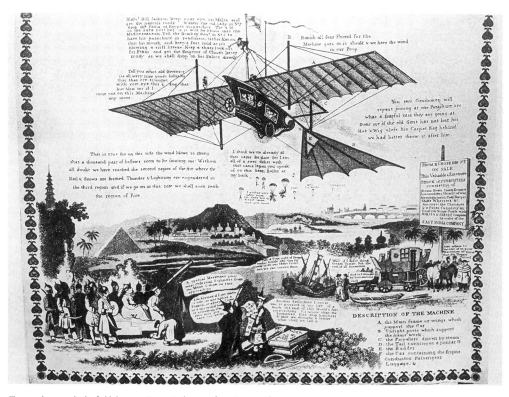

The popular press had a field day over Henson's dreams of starting an airline.

mocking cartoons. There was, however, a more positive article in *The Times* of 30 March 1843, which concludes that '. . . possession of the long-coveted power of flight may now be safely anticipated'.

Henson and Stringfellow worked together on a new 20 foot model, but by 1845 Henson was losing his enthusiasm. Eventually he got married, emigrated to America, and patented a new safety razor. Stringfellow was left to carry on alone, and when the new model was finished he got workmen to carry it up to Bala Down for testing. He was so upset by people making fun of his work that he did this secretly, at night, and tried the first flight under cover of darkness. It was a disaster – the silk covering of the wings got wet

with dew, and became so heavy that the machine could not fly. He tried again in the daytime, day after day, every day for seven weeks, but finally had to admit defeat.

And then, for the first time, he designed his own aircraft from scratch. Accounts are few, but we know that it had a 10 foot wingspan, with swallow-shaped wings, rather than Henson's rectangular design. The wing area was about 18 sq. feet, and its overall weight perhaps 9 lb including the super-lightweight steam engine.

Stringfellow flew his plane for the first time in the summer of 1848, inside the top floor of a lace mill, some 20 metres long. Outside he had had trouble with damp and with cross-winds. His aircraft had no fin, nor anything else to prevent it from veering left or right. So flying it inside, in still air, seemed a good plan. He launched it along a fixed wire, which ran down a slight slope for nearly half the length of the mill; when the aircraft reached the end of the wire it released itself by a cunning catch. The wire launch enabled him to get a good smooth downhill run, so that by the time the machine started flying it was already moving at a reasonable speed, and was also flying exactly level, with no tendency to veer left or right. This last point was important, because the mill has a row of iron pillars down the middle, which means that the flight path was only about 20 feet wide; there was only 5 feet of clearance on either side.

In the first experiment, according to his son Fred, writing fifty years later, the tail was set at too high an angle, and the machine rose too rapidly on leaving the wire. After going a few yards it stalled and slid back as if down an inclined plane; the point of the tail struck the ground and was broken. Once the tail was repaired it was set at a lower angle. The steam was again got up, the machine started down the wire and upon reaching the point of self-detachment, gradually rose until it reached the farther end of the room, punching a hole in the canvas placed to stop it before it hit the wall.

This sketchy account is all we have, but several local worthies were there to witness this first powered flight, achieved by John Stringfellow in 1848.

19. SIR GEORGE CAYLEY, INVENTOR OF THE AEROPLANE

The world's first powered flight was achieved by John Stringfellow in 1848, but his aircraft was only a model. The first heavier-than-air flying machine to carry a person was built by another Yorkshireman, Sir George Cayley, and the epic flight took place in Brompton Vale in North Yorkshire in 1853.

In the little church in Brompton, poet William Wordsworth married his childhood sweetheart Mary Hutchinson on 4 October 1802. There is even a theory that his famous poem about daffodils was written not in the Lake District, as is generally supposed, but at Brompton, where there are also daffodils under the trees by a lake. William and Mary must have noticed that just behind the little church is a great house, called Brompton Hall, but they probably didn't realise that even while they were being married, the squire was busy in his garden shed designing the world's first aeroplane.

George Cayley was born on 27 December 1773. His family had lived at Brompton Hall for generations. When he was nineteen his father died, and George became the sixth baronet – Sir George Cayley. So he had both money and time, although he also had an estate to manage. He was always interested in scientific observation. At the age of fifteen he was timing the beats of a crow's wing, and while he was at school he measured the rate of growth of his thumbnail; it grew just half an inch in one hundred days.

For many years he enjoyed a close relationship with his intelligent cousin Miss Phil, but in 1795 he married a difficult and brittle girl called Sarah Walker, the daughter of his tutor in Nottingham. Their relationship was generally uncomfortable, and he may well have come to build his aircraft because she made the atmosphere in the house so chilly, and his workshop provided a refuge.

By 1796 he was designing flying machines. From string, whalebone, and feathers he created little toy ornithopters that would fly when wound up. He went on to design toy gliders, modelling them roughly on the crow. He realised that flight involved two important factors – forward propulsion and lift – and that the two could be tackled separately. He came to the conclusion – as did Stringfellow and Henson forty years later – that birds could get lift without flapping. After all, many birds glide for long distances without a single flap, and without plummeting to the ground. Cayley set about investigating lift by using a whirling-arm machine.

Aerodynamic experiments are hard to control, because you have to organise a steady flow of air or wind speed, and he did this by the ingenious use of a whirling-arm. He made his experimental wing of about one square foot, which he reckoned was the area of a crow's wings, and fixed it to the end of a wooden arm three feet long, pivoted near the centre on a vertical rod, and nearly counterbalanced at the other end. He wound a string round the rod, passed the end over a pulley, and hung a weight from it. When he let go of the weight it would fall, pulling the rod round and making the arm whirl. By doing this indoors he could be sure the 'wing' was always moving at constant speed through the air.

According to legend, his wife would not have this apparatus in the house; so he waited his opportunity. Their first child, Anne, was due in 1796 and Sarah went to stay with her mother in Nottingham for her confinement. George immediately set up his whirling-arm apparatus on the top landing in the great staircase of the Hall, so that the weight had a clear 20 foot drop to the ground. He tried various angles for mounting the wing, and reckoned he got maximum lift at an angle of 6°. Then he built a glider, with the wings set at 6° up from the fuselage, and went out to test it in Brompton Vale, the field behind the house.

He was so delighted by how well it flew that he waxed lyrical about the flying machines of the future. He reckoned a glider would be the ideal way to get people down mountains: 'It was very pretty to see it sail down a steep hill, and it gave the idea that a larger instrument would be a better and safer conveyance down the Alps than even the sure-footed mule.'

He went on to design the best aerodynamic shape for slipping through the air, and planned an internal combustion engine to provide power. 'When we can get a hundred horsepower into a pint pot,' he wrote to *The Times*, 'man will be able to transport his family and possessions as readily by air as he now does by railway.' He asserted that flying was the future, and that we should all come to use 'that uninterrupted navigable ocean which comes to the threshold of every man's door. . . . We shall be able to transport ourselves and our families with their goods and chattels more securely by air than by water, and at a velocity of from 20 to 100 miles an hour.'

Unfortunately, for many years he was too busy to pursue flying. He invented rifling for the barrels of big guns. He suggested that passengers on trains should wear seat-belts. He designed a net like a cow-catcher to attach to the front of trains so that any workmen on the line would be scooped up rather than run over. He designed an 'Artificial hand for working men', and became MP for Scarborough. But in the 1840s he returned to aeronautics. He built a triplane which carried a boy off the ground on a downhill flight. And finally, in 1852, he built his New Flyer.

Cayley described his New Flyer in some detail in the *Mechanics* magazine of 15 September that year, although for some reason he gave the article the title 'Governable parachutes'. It was a monoplane with a kite-shaped wing and a tricycle undercarriage. In order to keep the weight down, Cayley had devised wheels with small rims and spokes of string in tension; in other words he had incidentally invented the bicycle wheel!

The following year, 1853, saw the first flight. Sir George was by now seventy-nine – rather old to be the world's first test-pilot – so he volunteered his coachman, probably one John Appleby, to take the tiller. The aircraft was launched from the grass field on the high east side of Brompton Vale by half a dozen farm hands running and pulling on ropes. It soared into the air, flew right across the valley – about 200 yards – and landed heavily on the grass the other side. The coachman clambered out of the wreckage, and said: 'Please, Sir George, I wish to give notice. I was hired to drive, not to fly!' Nevertheless, this was the world's first flight of a heavier-than-air person carrying aircraft.

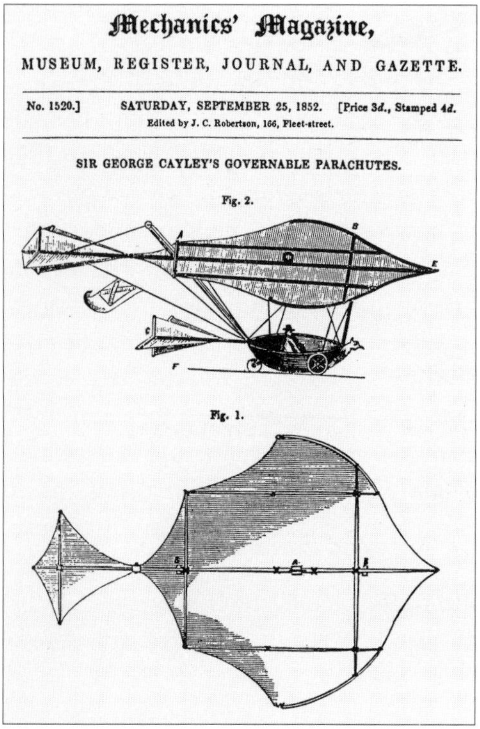

When the Wright brothers flew their aircraft *Flyer I* at Kittyhawk in North Carolina on 17 December 1903, they paid tribute to Cayley: 'About 100 years ago an English-man, Sir George Cayley, carried the science of flying to a point which it had never reached before and which it scarcely reached again during the last century.'

Sir George Cayley volunteered his coachman to be the world's first test-pilot.

Mechanics' Magazine,

MUSEUM, REGISTER, JOURNAL, AND GAZETTE.

No. 1520.]   SATURDAY, SEPTEMBER 25, 1852.   [Price 3d., Stamped 4d.
Edited by J. C. Robertson, 166, Fleet-street.

SIR GEORGE CAYLEY'S GOVERNABLE PARACHUTES.

Fig. 2.

Fig. 1.

The New Flyer of 1852.

In Brompton, 7 miles west of Scarborough, there's a pub called the Cayley Arms. Although Brompton Hall is now a school there is a plaque on the back of Cayley's workshop, visible from the road.

SEEING THE LIGHT

We interact in all sorts of ways with the world around us, but for most people by far the majority of information comes from vision. We rely on our eyes to tell us what's going on in the world, whether we're crossing the road, reading a newspaper, watching television – or simply reading this book! Because vision is so important, scientists have for hundreds of years wondered about how our eyes work, what light is, and how sight can be varied or improved. Here are just a few of the stories of those puzzlers.

20. DENNIS GABOR AND THE HOLOGRAM

This book is a monument to ingenuity and invention. One of the intriguing aspects of the subject is how people have original ideas – specifically where and when their flashes of inspiration arrive. Sometimes the genius tells us, and the occasions are varied and curious. William Watts dreamed up how to make lead shot while lying in a stupor by his local church. Edward Berthon was sketching on Lake Geneva; Isaac Newton was allegedly sitting in his garden 'in contemplative mood', and there are many other examples. Perhaps the nearest we can get to a common set of conditions is that the person is doing something rather ordinary, something that takes time but little mental effort, so that the brain is free to roam . . . The Greek scientist Archimedes had one of his brilliant ideas in the bath, and leapt out shouting 'Eureka!' Unfortunately he was in the public bath in Syracuse, and he must have caused a few heads to turn as he ran home stark-naked. On the morning of 12 September 1933 Leo Szilard was waiting for the traffic lights to change so that he could cross Southampton Row on the corner of Russell Square in London. As he stepped off the kerb he suddenly realised, in a flash, how it might be possible to start a nuclear chain reaction, and so make atom bombs.

Dennis Gabor said he got most of his ideas while he was shaving, and he supposed that men with beards have fewer ideas, but the inspiration that won him the Nobel Prize came to him in 1947 while he was sitting at St Andrews Tennis Club in Rugby, waiting to play tennis with Winifred Smith. The previous players finished, and gathered their things. Miss Smith got up expectantly, but Dennis muttered something about having to check out an idea, and wandered off, leaving her without an opponent!

Gabor had just conceived the idea of the hologram – that a coherent light beam would carry three-dimensional information when it reflected from an object, and so in principle could produce a three-dimensional image. Unfortunately there was no practical coherent light source in 1947, so holograms could not be made until the laser was invented more than ten years later. Yet now we have holograms on every credit card, thanks to that flash of inspiration by a tennis court.

Every credit card hologram is a tribute to Dennis Gabor. St Andrews Tennis Club in Bilton Road, Rugby, is now a funeral parlour, but there is a plaque on his house at 47A Bilton Road.

21. ALL DONE BY MIRRORS: DAVID BREWSTER AND THE KALEIDOSCOPE

The kaleidoscope, that perennial Christmas stocking filler, was discovered by accident in 1816. The circumstances were so trivial – you only need two mirrors at an angle – that it is surprising no one had found the effect before. But the man playing with mirrors happened to be one of the greatest optical theoreticians of the nineteenth century, Sir David Brewster (1781–1868).

Brewster was the sort of scientist who simply could not exist today. Born in the Scottish Borders, he went to university at the age of twelve (not so unusual at the time) and became a minister in the Church. However, he got so nervous about having to give sermons that sometimes he fainted, so he gave it up, became a tutor, and studied science in his spare time. He became a popular science writer, editor of a magazine and an encyclopaedia, and published many papers on optics. Although he started out as an amateur, he was knighted, made a fellow of the Royal Society, and ended up as Principal of Edinburgh University.

His main research was on polarised light, and he is remembered for inventing the Brewster Angle: the angle at which light strikes a particular surface to give maximum polarisation. One day he was experimenting with an 'optical trough', a long trough with triangular ends and mirrors for sides. He was known for his fine practical work, but this time he was a bit careless and got a blob of glue on the mirrors where they joined. He was surprised to see that the ugly blob formed a rather beautiful flower-like pattern. He realised it must be something to do with the angle between the mirrors. He found that as the angle increased, he got a succession of these symmetrical images, whenever the angle would go exactly into 360°. He named his invention the 'Kaleidoscope' from the Greek for 'beautiful form', and patented it. He also wrote a long and rather tedious treatise on the use of the device, which he reckoned would be good for designing things like carpets. Sadly for Brewster, his patent was not watertight, so others hijacked the idea, and the kaleidoscope was all the rage. Interestingly, the early kaleidoscopes were made with two mirrors. The triangular version came later.

Sir David Brewster, as seen with his invention, the kaleidoscope.

David Brewster lived in Melrose, where there is a lovely ruined abbey. His best memorial is the kaleidoscope which he invented.

22. THE DISCOVERY OF COAL GAS BY JOHN CLAYTON

For hundreds of years people must have been digging coal out of the ground and burning it for warmth. During all that time someone must surely have noticed that coal produces a flammable gas when it is heated. However, we have a precise date and location for the first scientific examination of the phenomenon, for John Clayton wrote an excited letter about it to Robert Boyle and the Royal Society published it in their *Philosophical Transactions*.

Within two miles of Wigan, he says, he found a ditch wherein the water seemed to burn like brandy, and the flame was so fierce that several strangers boiled eggs on it. What a wonderful discovery, on an afternoon walk, this assembly of egg-boiling strangers huddled around a ditch!

Determined to get to the bottom of this, he drained the ditch, dug down, and found some 'shelly coal'. He lit a candle and lowered it down the hole, and 'the air catched fire, and continued burning'.

So he took some of the coal home with him, heated it in a retort over his fire, and

---

[59]

the Tumour as opened : In both the Artift has fo far imployed his Care and Skill, as well in preferving the juft Dimenfions as in the Colours and Appearances, that I am left only to wifh, that in the Defcription, which I have made, my Pen had not fallen fhort of his Pencil.——I am, with the greateft Refpect,

SIR,

*Your moft obliged
humble Servant,*

Jer. Peirce.

V. *An Experiment concerning the* Spirit *of* Coals, *being part of a Letter to the Hon.* Rob. Boyle, *Efq; from the late Rev.* John Clayton, *D. D. communicated by the Right Rev. Father in God* Robert Lord Bifhop *of* Corke *to the Right Hon.* John Earl *of* Egmont, *F. R. S.*

——HAving feen a Ditch within two Miles from *Wigan* in *Lancafhire,* wherein the Water would feemingly burn like Brandy, the Flame of which was fo fierce, that feveral Strangers have boiled Eggs over it ; the People thereabouts indeed affirm, that about 30 Years ago it would have boiled a Piece of Beef ; and that whereas much Rain formerly made it burn much fiercer, now after Rain it would fcarce burn at all. It was after a long-con-
H 2   tinued

[60]

tinued Seafon of Rain that I came to fee the Place, and make fome Experiments, and found accordingly, that a lighted Paper, though it were waved all over the Ditch, the Water would not take Fire. I then hired a Perfon to make a Dam in the Ditch, and fling out the Water, in order to try whether the Steam which arofe from the Ditch would then take Fire, but found it would not. I ftill, however, purfued my Experiment, and made him dig deeper ; and when he had dug about the Depth of half a Yard, we found a fhelly Coal, and the Candle being then put down into the Hole, the Air catched Fire, and continued burning.

I obferved that there had formerly been Coal-pits in the fame Clofe of Ground ; and I then got fome Coal from one of the Pits neareft thereunto, which I diftilled in a Retort in an open Fire. At firft there came over only *Phlegm,* afterwards a black *Oil,* and then likewife a *Spirit* arofe, which I could noways condenfe, but it forced my Lute, or broke my Glaffes. Once, when it had forced the Lute, coming clofe thereto, in order to try to repair it, I obferved that the Spirit which iffued out caught Fire at the Flame of the Candle, and continued burning with Violence as it iffued out, in a Stream, which I blew out, and lighted again, alternately, for feveral times. I then had a Mind to try if I could fave any of this Spirit, in order to which I took a turbinated Receiver, and putting a Candle to the Pipe of the Receiver whilft the Spirit arofe, I obferved that it catched Flame, and continued burning at the End of the Pipe, though you could not difcern what fed the Flame : I then blew it out, and lighted it again feveral times ; after
which

Part of John Clayton's letter.

Making gas while the sun shines: the church roof at Crofton seems to have been repaired by John Clayton, so it seemed a fitting place to repeat his coal-gas experiment, assisted by the rector – Clayton's successor.

watched with fascination. At first came only phlegm, then black oil – he was founding the chemical industry here – and then a gas which he collected and stored in bladders, and was able to ignite and amaze his friends. This flammable gas was coal gas which, when the technology became available, provided light and some power for Victorian England.

The evidence is patchy, but he may have been the same John Clayton who was Rector of Crofton near Wakefield from 1687 to 1694, and went on to become a bishop in Ireland. He repaired the church roof and the steeple in 1689 – and seems to have discovered coal gas in his spare time!

John Clayton's name is on the list of rectors of Crofton Church, south-east of Wakefield.

23. SOHO BY GASLIGHT BY WILLIAM MURDOCH

More than a hundred years after the discovery of coal gas the technology was invented to allow it to be exploited. The first person to suggest seriously that it should be used for lighting was an amazing but largely unknown Scotsman, William Murdoch. At home in 1772 he had apparently found that he could make coal gas by heating coal in his mother's teapot; he realised that in principle coal gas could be used to make bright reliable lighting. His chance came in Birmingham.

He was always inventive; as a boy he had built a wooden tricycle to ride to school with his brothers in Ayrshire – and this was decades before even the hobbyhorse. He designed a new type of lathe, and used it to make himself an oval wooden hat.

William Murdoch, gas light pioneer, who may have changed his name to Murdock (with a k) so that the English would pronounce it correctly.

William Murdock's original gasholder of 1798 installed at the Soho Foundry, Boulton & Watt's great steam engine factory. Murdock ran the works and lived on site.

In 1777 he went to Birmingham to apply for a job with the great engineering firm of Boulton & Watt. Boulton would have turned him away, but Murdoch was wearing his oval hat – and got the job. Eventually he became the Third Man in the Boulton & Watt empire, and he stayed with the firm for fifty-three years. They sent him off to look after their steam engine interests in Cornwall, where he annoyed his landlady by hanging fish to dry all round his room. In 1784 he built a model steam locomotive, but Boulton & Watt didn't want to know – in fact they actively discouraged him from pursuing such a frivolity – and his Cornish acquaintance Richard Trevithick built the first working steam locomotive about fifteen years later.

When Murdoch returned to Birmingham he lived in a cottage in the Soho foundry where they started making their own steam engines after Watt's patent had expired in 1800. There he picked up and developed his idea of gas lighting; he lit his house with it, and by 1802 he had installed gas lighting through the entire Soho manufactory. But still it came to nothing. Unfortunately Boulton refused to patent gas lighting; he said they had enough patents already what with their steam engines and so on, and so Murdoch never made a penny out of his brightest ideas.

William Murdoch's cottage, marked by a plaque, still stands in the remains of the Soho Foundry in Birmingham, now part of the Avery Works.

24. GOLDSWORTHY GURNEY: BRIGHT LIGHT, AND EXHAUSTING HOT AIR

Candles and gas lamps produced a feeble, yellowish, flickering glow, just about bright enough to read by, but hardly enough to fill a large room with light. The first really bright light was invented by a Cornishman called Goldsworthy Gurney. He was an enterprising and energetic man, who was born on 14 February 1793 at Padstow, had a medical practice before he was twenty, married a farmer's daughter the next year, and moved to London in 1820. Thereafter he divided his time between London, where he could be part of Society, and the north Cornish seaside town of Bude, where in the early 1830s he built himself a castle. It's still there, standing on a concrete raft on a sand dune, close to where the canal empties on to the beach. Today it's the town hall.

Allegedly he lit the whole of his castle with a single central lamp, reflecting light into every room with carefully placed mirrors. This was clever, but what was really revolutionary was the light itself, for it was far brighter than any lamp had been before. Gurney achieved this by blowing oxygen into the flame, thus ensuring rapid and complete combustion of the fuel. In 1823 he had been awarded the Isis gold medal of the Royal Society of Arts for his invention of the oxygen-hydrogen blowpipe, and his 'Bude Light' was really just a practical extension of the same idea, though he did not patent it until 1839.

Bude Lights were used to brighten the streets of London – notably Trafalgar Square and Pall Mall – and in 1839 Gurney was invited to improve the lighting in the House of Commons. He did so in a dramatically simple way, by removing 280 candles, and replacing them with just three Bude Lights, which successfully lit the place for sixty years, until electricity came along around the turn of the century. But Gurney's bright thoughts went further than this, for in 1864 he wrote a paper outlining how seamen might identify lighthouses; he proposed that each lighthouse should have a Bude Light in a revolving frame, so that from anywhere out at sea it would flash on and off at regular intervals. By varying the number of flashes and the intervals between them, each lighthouse could have its own signature; thus a sailor who was sailing along the coast at night could quickly work out his exact position. Now, for example, the Eddystone Lighthouse shows two flashes every ten seconds, while the Bishop Rock Lighthouse shows two flashes every fifteen seconds.

Gurney's most spectacular invention – and the one that cost him most money – was the steam carriage. He had come up with the idea of the high-pressure steam jet, probably as yet another by-product of the oxygen-hydrogen jet, which greatly increased the efficiency of steam engines, and was apparently adopted by the Stephensons in their famous locomotives. Gurney, however, decided to use it to build a steam carriage, which he patented in 1825. He simply removed the horses from the front of an ordinary coach, and replaced them with a steam engine. At first he put the boiler under the passenger seats, but realised this might inspire terror, and in 1828 designed and built a

Goldsworthy Gurney's steam carriage.

Drag – a separate engine to pull the coach.

In 1826 he gave up his successful medical practice to develop the Gurney Steam Carriage Company, and in November 1827 the *Gentleman's Magazine* announced 'A steam-coach company is now making arrangements for stopping places on the line of road between London, Bath, and Bristol, which will occur every six or seven miles, where fresh fuel and water are to be supplied. There are fifteen coaches built.'

In 1829 Gurney was asked by the Quartermaster-General of the Army to lay on an official demonstration, in the shape of a journey from London to Bath and back. They set off at the dead of night on 27 July for what proved to be quite an adventure. After less than a mile, while crossing over a temporary bridge, they managed to collide with the Bristol mail-coach, and had to repair the damage in Reading. They were attacked by a Luddite mob in Melksham and had to cover the last few miles to Bath under guard. After four days' rest they returned home, completing the round trip at an average speed of 15 mph, much faster than the mail-coach. This was the first long journey at a maintained speed by any mechanised vehicle.

Two weeks later, on 12 August, the Duke of Wellington, then Prime Minister, asked for a demonstration in Hounslow Barracks, where the Drag first pulled the duke's carriage around the yard, and later a wagon carrying twenty-seven soldiers.

Sir Charles Dance started a regular steam carriage service between Cheltenham and Gloucester – covering the 9 miles four times a day – which ran for five months in 1831 until it was sabotaged by the mail-coach owners. However, despite this and other triumphs, the steam carriage failed to carry the day. The government decided to back the rapidly developing railways with an Exchequer Loan of £100,000, but rushed through a series of Turnpike Bills which put prohibitive tolls on horseless carriages. Gurney protested, and petitioned Parliament, but in 1832 his business failed; he had to abandon the whole thing, and lost £232,000.

One thing Gurney must have known as well as anyone was that politicians produce a great deal of hot air. In the 1850s MPs kept falling asleep, and in 1854 Gurney was appointed Inspector of Ventilation at the Houses of Parliament. He sorted them out with one of his steam jets, and went on to develop the Gurney Stove for warming and moisturizing air; it was used in many cathedrals.

His steam jets were also used to put out a fire in a coal mine at Clackmannan that had been burning for thirty years, and to clean out a revolting sewer at Friar Street.

In 1863 he was knighted by Queen Victoria, and in 1875 he died. His daughter, a fanatical supporter, donated a memorial chiming clock to the church at Poughill on the north side of Bude. It's a pretty stone church, with chickens in the graveyard, the nice blue clock on the tower, and a strong bell-ringing tradition. There's an excellent plaque inside the church above the door, describing with only slight exaggeration why he was a hero: 'His inventions and discoveries in steam and electricity rendered transport by land and sea so rapid that it became necessary for all England to keep uniform clock time.'

Goldsworthy Gurney's castle is now Bude Town Hall.

25. ISAAC NEWTON AND THE COLOURS OF THE RAINBOW

Isaac Newton can't have enjoyed a happy childhood. Born at the full moon in the early hours of Christmas Day 1642 – the year that Galileo had died – he was so tiny at birth they said he would have fitted into a quart pot, and so sickly looking that he was not expected to survive the night. His father had died a few months earlier, and three years later his mother went off to marry a rich clergyman, leaving the baby in the not-so-tender care of her strict parents. When her new husband died she returned to the family home, Woolsthorpe Manor, but found Isaac an awkward lad. She wanted his help on the farm, but he was happier at the King's School in Grantham, where there is still an I. NEWTON carved in large crooked capitals on a window-sill in what is now the library. He was a dreamy lad, and the tale is told that usually he daydreamed on his way home from the market in Grantham. Everyone had to get off their horses and walk up Spitalgate Hill, but Isaac often forgot to get on again at the top, and would walk the 5 miles home, leading his horse.

He went off to Cambridge in 1661, but in April 1665 the University was closed because of an outbreak of plague. So Isaac went home, and with only himself for company, and his mind free to wander, he began the most productive and imaginative eighteen months of his life, 'for in those years I was in the prime of my age for invention, and minded Mathematics and Philosophy more than at any time since'. During that fertile period he not only invented the basis of

Woolsthorpe Manor, south of Grantham, where Isaac Newton was born, and spent his *annus mirabilis.*

calculus and solved several major mathematical problems, he also unearthed the basic principle of gravity, and set up in his head the fundamental laws of motion – although he did not write them down for another twenty years! And he solved the enigma of the spectrum.

We think we know how he set about this, because he wrote a wonderfully explicit letter to the Royal Society which describes in detail his experiments, his observations, and his conclusions. 'In the beginning of 1666,' he writes, 'I procured me a triangular glass-prisme, to try therewith the celebrated *phenomena* of *colours*.' Then, 'having darkened my chamber, and made a small hole in my window-shuts, to let in a convenient quantity of the sun's light, I placed my

prisme at his entrance, that it might be thereby refracted to the opposite wall.' He was delighted at the pretty and intense colours, and he soon noticed that although his hole was round, the spectrum was five times as long as it was broad, 'a disproportion so extravagant, that it excited me to a more than ordinary curiosity of examining, from whence it might proceed'.

He first checked that this elongation was not produced by thickness or irregularity in the glass, or other similar simple anomaly, and then he wondered whether the rays of light were curving through the air, 'when I remembered that I had often seen a tennis ball, struck with an oblique racket, describe such a curve line'. But he satisfied himself that this was not the case. And so he was led to his crucial experiment: 'The gradual removal of these suspicions at length led me to the *Experimentum Crucis*, which was this: I took two boards, and placed one of them close behind the prisme at the window, so that the light might pass through a small hole . . . and fall on the other board, which I placed at about 12 feet distance, having first made a small hole in it also, for some of the incident light to pass through. Then I placed another prisme behind this second board, so that the light, trajected through both the boards, might pass through that also, and be again refracted before it arrived at the wall.'

What he found was that when he let a ray of red light through his second prism it was refracted again before it reached the back wall. When he let through a ray of blue light it too was refracted again,

but much more than the red. Thus it was clear to him that light of different colours was refracted through different angles, the blue more than the red. Furthermore, each colour he let through did not break up into new colours, but 'obstinately retained its colour, notwithstanding my utmost endeavours to change it'.

He concluded that white light is not a single colour, but can only be a mixture of colours. Therefore the prism produces colours from white light because it refracts the different colours by different amounts, and so separates them one from another. 'Why the colours of the rainbow appear in falling drops of rain, is also from hence evident. For those drops, which refract the rays, disposed to appear purple . . . are the drops on the inside of the primary bow, and on the outside of the secondary or exterior one . . . those drops, which refract . . . red . . .

A Letter of Mr. Isaac Newton, *Professor of the Mathematicks in the University of Cambridge; containing his New Theory about* Light *and* Colors : *sent by the Author to the Publisher from Cambridge,* Febr. 6. $16\frac{21}{72}$; *in order to be communicated to the* R. Society.

S I R,

TO perform my late promise to you, I shall without further ceremony acquaint you, that in the beginning of the Year 1666 (at which time I applyed my self to the grinding of Optick glasses of other figures than *Spherical*,) I procured me a Triangular glass-Prisme, to try therewith the celebrated *Phænomena* of

G g g g   *Colours.*

The opening of Isaac Newton's February 1672 letter to the Royal Society.

are the drops on the exterior part of the primary, and interior part of the secondary bow.'

In the middle of this long letter he diverts for a page or so to explain why this varied refraction of light of different colours will lead to coloured fringes in telescope images, since the focal length of a lens must vary from colour to colour. And he goes on to describe the reflecting telescope he built to avoid this problem, and through which he had seen the moons of Jupiter. Thus the Newtonian telescope first appeared in print as an aside in his letter about the spectrum!

Much of this fascinating letter reads as though he has just come from the experiments on the bench; the descriptions are so simple and fresh. And yet this is far from the case. For one thing he says at the beginning 'I procured me a triangular glass-prisme' – according to legend he bought it at Stourbridge Fair near Cambridge – but then a few pages later he introduces 'another prisme', so he can't just have gone to the fair and bought one. . . . What's more, he wrote this letter to the Royal Society in February 1672. The telescopic work was fresh, but six years had gone by since his first prism experiments, he had become Lucasian Professor of Mathematics at Cambridge, and he had delivered at least one course of lectures on optics; so by then the spectral ideas were firmly established in his mind, and there must have been plenty of hindsight to guide his precise descriptions.

However, when this letter was published, Newton was attacked by his rival Robert Hooke, who cast doubt on Newton's conclusions, and said the crucial experiment did not work. To be fair, the light becomes very faint after going through two holes and two prisms, so that making objective observations is extremely difficult; you can easily convince yourself that you can see what you want to see!

Newton was furious at being attacked in this way, and almost vowed never to publish his results again. Indeed he avoided publishing anything apart from a brief tract *Propositiones de Motu* until his great book *Philosophiae Naturalis Principia Mathematica* came out fifteen years later, in 1687. He published nothing more on light until Hooke had died, and his book *Opticks*, published in 1704, contains no mention of the phrase *'Experimentum Crucis'*!

Science is rarely simple, and even Isaac Newton could not solve the mystery of the colours of the rainbow without bitter argument. For most of his life, Newton was cantankerous and self-obsessed, but occasionally he produced bursts of charm. Writing a conciliatory letter to Hooke, he said: 'If I have seen further, it is by standing on the shoulders of giants.' And near the end of his life he said: 'I do not know how I may appear to the world, but to myself I seem only like a boy playing on the seashore, and diverting myself in now and then finding a smoother pebble or a prettier shell than ordinary, while the great ocean of truth lay all undiscovered before me.'

Isaac Newton's home, Woolsthorpe Manor, 5 miles south of Grantham, is open to the public on some days during the summer. Beware, there are two Woolsthorpes; Albert Einstein went to the wrong one! There is Newton Way and Newton Lane, and in Grantham the Isaac Newton Shopping Centre and material in Grantham Museum; 01476 568783.

26. THREE MEN, ONE VISION: DALTON, YOUNG, MAXWELL AND THE PROBLEM OF COLOUR BLINDNESS

Although experiments have become the supreme test of scientific ideas, there are times when an experiment simply cannot be done. This is especially true where the human body is concerned: if you start taking it apart, it quite often stops working. The solution is to wait until the body performs an experiment on itself. The nature of colour, and how we see it, is a problem that intrigued scientists for generations. Three of Britain's greatest physical scientists, all working outside their main field of interest, were involved in finding the answers, and all of them realised that colour-blindness was the key. Each built upon the work of his predecessor, and the result was not only an understanding of how we see colour, but the first colour photograph.

The first of the three was John Dalton (1766–1844). He was born in the village of Eaglesfield, in Cumbria. The plaque on the outside of the house describes him as the 'founder of the atomic theory', but this hardly does justice to his extraordinary life. The Lake District seems to have been a haven for radical scientists like Dalton and the extraordinary John Gough, the blind botanist written about by Wordsworth. Gough was Dalton's teacher, and Dalton himself became a teacher at the age of twelve. Both men were Quakers, a religion popular in the north west, but not well tolerated in the established universities of Oxford and Cambridge, where you had to sign the Articles of the Church of England if you wanted to study. As a result, Dalton developed his scientific thinking away from the mainstream.

Dalton's work on colour-blindness was a sideline. The work for which he is famous is the atomic theory, which really began on 27 March 1787, when he saw the northern lights – the aurora borealis – and wrote an account of his observations in a meteorological journal. He kept up his journal for fifty-seven years, and in all recorded about 200,000 observations. He said himself in later life that his book of meteorological observations and essays contained the germs of most of the later ideas he worked on.

A lesser man might have been happy to leave it at that, but in thinking about the atmosphere, Dalton realised that current ideas did not properly account for the way particles combined. As a weather fanatic he was interested in air pressure, and wondered how all the gases in the atmosphere might combine to make up the total pressure. His then radical answer was that they did not interact at all, but that the total pressure is made up of the 'partial pressures' of each gas, which is the same as it would be if all the other gases were not present. He also noticed that when you dissolve gas in water, the water will take up a different weight of each gas. He concluded not only that the 'elementary particles' of each gas were different weights, and calculated the relative weights of the atoms of different elements, but went on to show how chemistry was governed by the way these atoms combine. This staggering achievement was only gradually recognised. Humphry Davy at first objected, but then declared the atomic theory 'the greatest scientific advance of recent times'.

Botany was an important pastime, no doubt inspired by Gough. However, Dalton noticed that he and his brother described flowers differently from others. His detailed description of his condition to the Manchester Literary and Philosophical Society constitutes the first scientific account of colour-blindness. In it he suggested that the problem might be in the humours of the eye – the transparent fluids that fill the spaces in the eyeball. He could account for his inability to distinguish colours properly if at least one of the humours was stained deep blue, preventing red light from reaching his retina. He gave directions that after his death his eyes were to be dissected to see if this was true.

Dalton was much respected, though not well liked. Davy wrote of him: 'Mr. Dalton's aspect and manner were repulsive. There was no gracefulness belonging to him. His voice was harsh and brawling; his gait stiff and awkward, his style of writing and conversation dry and almost crabbed.' Dalton moved to Manchester in later life, where despite his personal qualities, he was a real hero. When he died his body lay in state in Manchester Town Hall and some forty thousand people came to pay their respects. His wish to have his eyes dissected was carried out – but the humours were found to be quite transparent.

Thomas Young (1773–1829) carried the thinking much further. Young was as multi-talented as Dalton, working not only on how the eye focuses and sees colour, but on many medical theories as well as studying materials science, and helping to translate the Rosetta Stone! His most far-reaching work was probably the wave theory of light. And he did all this while practising medicine, and regretted that he wasn't taken more seriously as a doctor. Young knew about Dalton's ideas – and rejected them. He suggested instead that the eye might

Thomas Young measured the length of his own eyeball.

contain regions sensitive to different colours – he at first thought red, blue and yellow but later settled on red, green and violet. He thought that colour-blindness could be

Thomas Young provided the key to translating the Rosetta Stone when he realised that the hieroglyphic, demotic and Greek sections were all carrying the same message.

James Clerk Maxwell holding one of his colour wheels.

A colour wheel belonging to James Clerk Maxwell, and used on normal and colour-blind volunteers to show that the eye uses red, green and blue receptors for colour vision.

better explained not by a stain in the humour of the eye, but by some fault in one of these sensitive areas. He could not have known in 1801 what the structures might be, and he died before Dalton, so he did not know the result of the post-mortem. It was a bravura piece of theoretical biology.

One of Young's tools was taken up by the third scientific giant to tackle colour-blindness, James Clerk Maxwell (1831–79). A scientific prodigy, Maxwell had written his first scientific paper when he was only fourteen. Young had suggested the use of a colour-wheel divided into segments, each of a different colour. When the wheel was spun, the colours appear to mix. Maxwell made elegant metal spinning-tops fitted with discs of coloured paper. They could be arranged so that more or less of any colour was visible. He would then spin the disc

and ask the viewer if the colour matched that of a reference. If not, the discs could be adjusted until the match was perfect. He found that most people could match white by mixing red, green and blue.

The beauty of the experiment was that colour-blind people could also match colours – except that they would do so *without using one of the coloured discs*. Most frequently they would achieve 'white' without using red. This showed that Young was right, and that colour-blindness is probably due to the inability to perceive one of the primary colours.

In 1863, having discovered that the eye can be tricked into seeing any colour with red, green and blue light, Maxwell used black and white film and coloured filters to take the first colour photo-graph. His demonstration that light is part of an electromagnetic spectrum is one of the keystones of modern physics. Final proof of the way we see colour came in 1946. A tiny beam of white light was shone into the eye. As it moved over the cells of the retina, it appeared red, green or blue.

Dalton's birthplace still stands at Eaglesfield near Cockermouth; the James Clerk Maxwell Foundation at 14 India Street, Edinburgh is open on request – 0113 220 1777; the Rosetta Stone is on display in the British Museum.

Glenlair, Maxwell's home in south-west Scotland, where he invented colour photography.

27. ALLOWING DUFFERS TO DRAW: THE SQUEAMISH BUT BRILLIANT WILLIAM HYDE WOLLASTON

Some heroes come up with a single idea or invention; others are incredibly versatile. Here is a man who in the early 1800s produced fifty-six scientific papers, on subjects ranging from fairy rings in the garden to dark lines in the spectrum of the sun, and why the eyes of a portrait on the wall seem to follow you around the room. He made a fortune from platinum. He invented the reflecting goniometer and a telescopic blowpipe. He very nearly got the top job in British science. But the most appealing of all his achievements was the invention of a machine to help in sketching.

William Hyde Wollaston (1766–1828)

was born in East Dereham in Norfolk, and intended to be a doctor. Indeed he practised at Huntingdon and Bury St Edmunds before trying London, and setting up practice in the Strand. By then he was thirty-one and not doing as well as he would have liked; he failed to be appointed physician at St George's Hospital. In 1800 he retired from medicine. Some sources suggest that his reason for quitting was not annoyance over the St George's job, but that he had decided he was emotionally unsuited to being a doctor. On one occasion, as he told his friend Henry Hasted, he was so upset about a patient that he burst into tears. On 29 December 1800 he wrote: 'Allow me to decline the mental flagellation called anxiety, compared with which the loss of thousands of pounds is

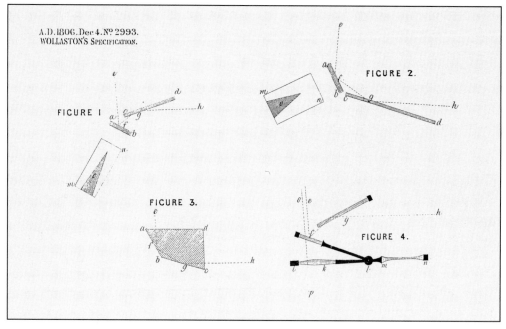

Wollaston realised there were many possible forms of Camera Lucida, and patented four different versions.

as a fleabite.' Keen to avoid all sources of stress, he vowed never to marry. Wollaston may have been happy, but he clearly realised that with his practice gone, he had to make some money.

He was already a Fellow of the Royal Society, and his desire to spend more time as a scientist must have helped him decide to quit medicine. He also worked out how to make money from what had been a hobby. He set up a laboratory in his house at 14 Buckingham Street, which he kept absolutely secret. He worked on platinum, which had caused real problems. It has a high melting-point, and is very resistant to chemical attack, so it ought to have been useful – but no one had found a way of making it into practical objects. Wollaston discovered a method, but did not reveal it until near the end of his life – by which time he had made £30,000.

Walking in the Lake District with Henry Hasted, a vicar and Fellow of the Royal Society, Wollaston decided to sketch the beautiful landscape. According to Hasted, Wollaston had extraordinary eyesight, being easily able to identify distant plants while on horseback. But he turned out to be a hopeless artist. So in 1807 he invented and patented the Camera Lucida. He seems to have invented the name also; the Camera Obscura was a well known artists' aid and amusement, consisting of a darkened room (the literal translation of 'Camera Obscura') or box with either a pinhole or lens in one wall, which projects an image of the outside world on to the opposite inside wall. Wollaston's device did not operate in the dark, which explains the use of 'Lucida', meaning light, but it isn't a box either.

Perhaps he just recognised the need for a marketable name.

Apparently his inspiration came from seeing a glass-topped table. He realised that it is possible to see simultaneously something reflected in the glass, and the floor beneath the table, and his patent details several devices which make use of this principle. The simplest version is just a piece of glass at an angle of 45°. You place the glass over your sketching pad and look down through the glass at the paper. You will see the pad as usual, and you will also be able to see the scene directly ahead of you, reflected into your eye by the surface of the glass. You then simply trace around the reflection with your pencil. This sounds brilliant, but in practice there are several problems, all of which Wollaston addressed. First, you will be drawing a mirror image of the real scene. Second, it appears upside down, which makes it almost impossible to glance from the sketch to the real subject to see how you are doing. Third it is impossible to focus on the pencil tip and the distant scene at the same time. Finally, if the scene is very bright or very dark, it may be difficult to see the pencil or the sketch 'through' it.

Wollaston's first improvement was to use two reflections. In front of the piece of glass, he attached a mirror. The angle between the two was to be 135°, and it was used in the same way as before – only now the reflection was the right way up, and correct from left to right. He tackled the focus difficulty with a magnifying lens under the piece of glass. The brightness problem was more tricky, but he came up with two solutions. The 'split mirror' Camera Lucida had a special mirror instead of the piece of glass. The silvering did not cover the whole surface: instead he applied it as a triangle. If you used the device near to your eye, the shape of the silvering was impossibly blurred, but the effect was to give a more or less reflective mirror depending upon whether you looked through the base or the pinnacle of the triangle. In this way you can alter the relative brightness of the sketch and subject. The commercial version used a dangerous-sounding 'split pupil' design, which used the same principle, except that you adjusted brightness by moving your eye over the *edge* of the mirror, so that some of your pupil looked at the mirror, some directly at the sketch.

Although the Camera Lucida and papers about fairy rings do not sound very serious, Wollaston was regarded as one of the leading scientific figures of his day. When the great Sir Joseph Banks died, he had been president of the Royal Society for forty-two years. He had wanted Wollaston to succeed him but Wollaston declined, knowing that Sir Humphry Davy wanted the job.

Charles Babbage, the great computer pioneer, occupied Wollaston's house after his death. He said of his friend that 'the most singular characteristic of Wollaston's mind was the plain and distinct line which separated what he knew from what he did not know . . . his predominant principle was to avoid error'. Among his contemporaries, he was known as 'the Pope'.

Wollaston's house stood in woodland behind what is now a private home in Dereham, Norfolk.

28. LET THERE BE LIGHT! JOSEPH WILSON SWAN AND THE PERFECTION OF THE ELECTRIC LIGHT BULB

Thomas Alva Edison probably deserves the title 'World's Greatest Inventor'. But despite his own claims and those of many American books, he did *not* invent the electric light bulb. That distinction belongs to Joseph Swan, a chemist from the north-east of England, working alone in his spare time. Swan and Edison both knew there were immense rewards for the man who succeeded in applying the new great power source, electricity, to the universal desire to light every home. The struggle to do so took place in the courts as well as the laboratory, but eventually saw the two men come together.

By 1850 gas lighting had been around for forty years, and was common in shops and posh homes, but gas was smelly, poisonous and expensive. It was not all that bright, either: the gas mantle you may have seen on camping-gas lights, which glows in the flame with an intense

Joseph Wilson Swan sees the light!

greenish-white light, was still a long way off. The gas lighting Swan and Edison would have known in their youth was a smoky yellow flame, so no wonder the new-fangled electricity seemed to offer the promise of a safer, cleaner light. In fact there was an electric light, the arc lamp – first used in Dungeness lighthouse in 1862. The arc lamp was an electric spark between two conducting rods connected to a battery. The trick lay in getting a constant arc, rather than spluttering sparks. This required the rods – usually of carbon – to be kept a constant distance apart, a problem since the rods are constantly burning away in the intense heat of the arc. In commercial applications, clever clockwork mechanisms were devised to first 'strike' the arc, by bringing the rods together, and then separating them to the right distance and maintaining the spark gap as the rods burned away.

These complications might have been overcome, but everyone knew the arc lamp would never become the universal electric light. Apart from the complexity, noise from the spark and the danger, arc lights were just too bright. If you had a lighthouse an arc lamp was fine, but as a bedside light it was seriously overpowered. However, the arc lamp defined the problem: it was rather quaintly called 'the subdivision of the electric light'.

Joseph Wilson Swan was born on 31 October 1828 at Pallion Hall in Sunderland. He left school when he was twelve, and was apprenticed to a firm of chemists, before taking up a position with John Mawson, a chemist in Newcastle. He invented several new processes for the developing photography business. In the 1840s Swan, a keen member of the Newcastle Literary and Philosophical Society, had seen a lecture at which electrical incandescence was demonstrated. A piece of wire was connected across a battery, and glowed orange. It was enough to make Swan think that incandescent lamps were the way to go. There is a problem: generally you either get no glow (wire too thick, battery too weak) or the wire burns out immediately. But if the wire survives, it is nowhere near bright enough to be a useful light. When the coil is glowing dull red, it's at about 700 or 800 °C. At about 1000° it would glow yellow, but then the copper would melt. Swan tried a mixture of platinum and iridium, and managed to get the temperature up to about 2000° before it melted, but he still wanted more.

So in his spare time from chemistry he experimented with all sorts of different materials. What we use now is the metal tungsten, but 130 years ago tungsten was both hard to obtain and impossible to work. So Swan chose carbon, which doesn't melt below 3500°. What he wanted was tiny thin pieces, which he made by taking little strips of paper and carbonising them by toasting them gently in an oven without air. He tried all sorts of paper, and he tried spreading them with treacle and syrup and other stuff that goes black when you overcook it. Some of these worked a bit, and glowed brightly, but they were still awfully weak: he could not get consistent success. Although carbon doesn't melt, it burns easily if there is any oxygen about.

The solution seemed obvious: get rid of the oxygen. He tried pumping all the air out of his bulbs with the mercury pump

that had just been invented, but this still did not work. There was enough oxygen adsorbed on the carbon – stuck to the outside – to burn it when it heated up. The stroke of genius which was to solve that problem took a while to come to Swan. Meanwhile, he tackled the unsatisfactory filaments themselves. He concluded that the fibrous nature of the paper he used was to blame, and decided to make his own material. The first artificial filaments were made by treating cotton with sulphuric acid, and later ones by dissolving blotting paper in zinc chloride and squirting it into alcohol to make long strings. These were in fact the first artificial fibres, precursors of rayon. He saw their potential, and asked his wife to crochet them into collars and doilies! They can be seen in the Newcastle Discovery museum.

By the late 1870s, when Swan had been working on the problem for a quarter of a century, everything was in place. He had his artificial filaments, carbonised in a furnace without air; the vacuum pump had been improved beyond recognition; and in 1878 he perfected a technique for getting rid of the adsorbed oxygen. When he had pumped all the air he could out of the glass bulb containing the filament, he carefully heated up the filament while still pumping. More oxygen came off the surface of the warm filament and was pumped away. For the first time, he could make his filament glow white, but not burn. He first demonstrated his successful lamp to a few people in January 1879, and then on 3 February 1879 to an audience of seven hundred people at the Literary and Philosophical Society of

Newcastle-upon-Tyne. Swan's house, Underhill at Gateshead, was lit with his own light bulbs later the same year.

He patented the pumping process, but he thought the idea of making a filament lamp so obvious it wasn't worth patenting. He reckoned without Thomas Alva Edison. Swan's lamp first worked in February 1879. Four months earlier Edison had made a dramatic, sweeping claim that he had solved the problem of the electric light by using carbonised paper. His cable sent the price of gas shares tumbling on the stock exchange – and in October 1879 Edison patented the carbon-filament lamp. Swan sent a little note to the journal *Nature* saying that he had been making carbonised paper

filaments for fifteen years – and it did not work. Edison went on to try fibres of carbonised bamboo, and imported it specially from Japan – but bamboo didn't work either.

In 1881 Swan started producing his carbon-filament light bulbs in a factory at Benwell, and Edison threatened to sue him for infringing his patent. Swan pointed out that he had been making these lamps before Edison applied for his patent. In the end they stopped arguing, joined forces, and formed the Edison & Swan United Electric Light Co.

Swan's most crucial work was done in the greenhouse at Underhill, his home in Gateshead, now a residential home for the elderly.

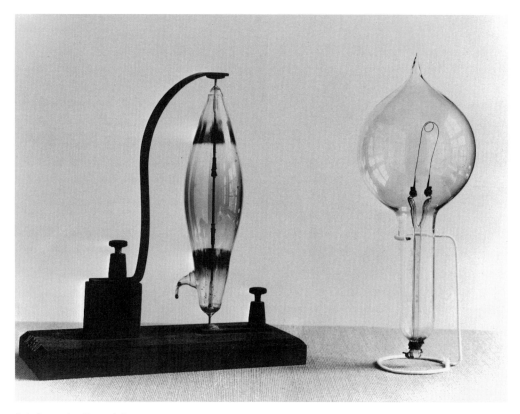

Early Swan carbon-filament bulbs.

THE BOWELS OF THE EARTH

Curiosity is probably the main driving force behind scientific enquiry; we long to find out how things work and what they are made of. We all live on this rocky planet, and a few of us have witnessed its more terrifying eruptions and earthquakes. Many scientists have devoted their lives to puzzling out some of its secrets; indeed the word 'scientist' was invented to describe some of the people mentioned in the stories below.

29. THE GIFTED AMATEUR: TEMPEST ANDERSON AND THE POWER OF VOLCANOES

Modern science does not seem to have much room for the amateur, a trend already established in the late nineteenth century. Dr Tempest Anderson (1846–1913), an eye surgeon from York who described himself as an 'amateur of limited leisure', was looking for a suitable scientific pastime. Curiously, he hit upon vulcanology – the study of volcanoes – because it offered 'exercise in the open air, often in districts remote and picturesque'. He intended to combine his new hobby with his other great love, photography. The result was a stunning record of dramatic eruptions from all over the world, and a new understanding of the destructive force of volcanoes.

Stonegate, one of the main streets of ancient York, is now filled with shops and tourists, but the elegant black and gold plaque outside no. 23 has survived: 'T. Anderson, Surgeon'. This is where Anderson practised as an ophthalmic surgeon, and is only yards from the house where he was born, at no. 17. But with a name like Tempest, he was never going to settle quietly. He used to keep two travel bags permanently packed, one for hot

'TA' was a roving vulcanologist with a roving eye: he had a knack for incorporating young women into his volcano pictures.

climates and one for cold. When word came of an eruption, he was off on the first available ship. There is no record of what happened to the patients in his waiting-room.

The idea of going to an erupting volcano by ship seems a bit daft: surely by the time news reached York, and Anderson had reached the volcano, it would all be over? In fact Anderson captured many eruptions on film, but his pictures of the aftermath of eruptions are just as powerful. The pictures are especially impressive when you consider the extraordinary lengths photographers routinely went to in those days. Wet plates, where you had to sensitise the glass photographic plate immediately before exposure by dipping it into silver-nitrate solution, had begun to disappear in 1874, the year after Anderson qualified as an MD, so he would have used dry plates for most of his work. But he would have taken hundreds of these glass plates with him on an expedition, together with several wooden cameras, many of which he made himself. Not only would he have to haul the cameras, lenses and plates up mountains in dangerous and inhospitable circumstances, but once on location the plates would have to be loaded, inside a light-proof bag, into 'dark slides' to hold them in the camera. It is a tribute to the pioneers of photography that early pictures progressed beyond posed studio shots. Anderson was clearly a genial chap, who made friends wherever he went. His new friends are recorded on his glass negatives and lantern slides, which feature many pictures of young women. As well as recording them playing cricket on board ship and so on, Anderson

photographed many of these women up the mountain, posed in ridiculously unsuitable gear with an erupting volcano in the background.

Having fun was clearly part of the point, and Anderson brought back many rather non-PC stories from his travels. One picture records the famous 'Fainting Dog of Vulcano'. Several times a day this unfortunate beast was led into a cavern with a layer of heavy volcanic gases near the floor. To the apparent amusement of the tourists, it would faint, only to revive again when carried outside. Anderson also visited Yellowstone in the USA to photograph the geysers, and was amused by a tale of an unfortunate Chinaman. The enterprising chap had set up a laundry in a hut on a hot spring. When he tipped in his soap powder, it set off the dormant geyser, which exploded into life, taking the hut with it.

However, Anderson's purpose was serious, and he became a respected authority. He made a thorough and systematic study of volcanoes, calling it a 'clinical or bedside study'. He was especially impressed by the destructive power of volcanoes, and by a paradox that reminded him of the Alps. A keen alpinist and member of the Alpine Club, Anderson had examined trees felled by avalanches. He found that those furthest from the origin of the avalanche had only a light sprinkling of snow. He concluded that they had been knocked over not by the rush of snow, but by the powerful wind the avalanche creates. He arrived at the same conclusion when considering the devastating eruptions on Martinique. The eruption of Mont Pelée had destroyed the town of Saint-Pierre in 1902. When

The waterfront at St Pierre on Martinique, devastated by the 1902 eruption of Mont Pelée, and photographed by 'TA'. He explained how destruction on this scale could happen even though there is no evidence of lava.

The Bank was the most complete structure left standing in St Pierre.

Anderson arrived, the scene was one of complete destruction. The only building left standing was part of the bank, the only survivor a man incarcerated in the underground cells of the jail. Yet, as his photographs show, there was not much ash or lava in the town itself.

The 'ground surge', as he called it, seems to precede the main eruption, and as its name implies it hugs the slopes of the volcano, destroying buildings and trees in its path with more than hurricane force. Sometimes the ground surge contains small rock particles as well as hot gas, and is also known as a 'pyroclastic flow'.

Anderson's pictures are all preserved at the Yorkshire Museum in York. There are over five thousand negatives and slides, some of which were published in Anderson's book *Volcanic Studies in Many Lands*. Sadly the museum is not able to display them at present, which is a pity, because the photography is superb and the collection includes many self portraits of the bearded Anderson clearly enjoying himself. Although Anderson found much of science closed to amateurs, he was part of a long tradition of amateur science in York, where the Literary and Philosophical Society, of which Anderson became president, was perhaps the greatest scientific society in Britain; in 1831 its members had founded the British Association for the Advancement of Science.

Because he was a scientific photographer, Tempest Anderson was keen to use only standard lenses, which have an angle of view the same as that of the human eye, rather than telephoto lenses that would produce an odd perspective. This meant, of course, that he had to get closer to the eruption he was photographing – which increased the risk. A friend said, 'you know, Anderson, you are sure to be killed, but it will be such a very great satisfaction to you afterwards to think that it was in the cause of science'. Tempest Anderson died of fever in 1913, crossing the Red Sea on the way back from the Philippines, and is buried at Suez.

Tempest Anderson's home was at 17 Stonegate, York, with his surgery just up the road at no. 23 Stonegate, York; there is still a plaque on a pillar.

30. JOHN MACKERETH'S PNEUMATIC BOTTOM CORER

The Lake District is a strikingly beautiful area of Britain, with majestic hills separated by lovely lakes. For decades the lakes have been used for recreation – they were the base for *Swallows and Amazons* and other Arthur Ransome sailing books. However, the lakes are also an important scientific resource, since they act as giant measuring and recording instruments. Flowing into Windermere, for example, are three rivers, and dozens of little streams. Together they bring down sediment from a catchment area of nearly 100 square miles. The mud on the bottom of the lake is formed partly from decaying aquatic plant and animal life, and leaves and insects that fall in, but mainly from all the silt that is carried down into the lake by these rivers. Each year a new layer is added to last year's sediment, until each year's mud is squashed down to a layer a fraction of a millimetre thick. So although the bottom of Windermere may look just like a sea of mud, in fact it's an ecological history book.

In order to read this book, ecologists need to take core samples. Essentially they push a hollow tube like a piece of drainpipe straight down into the mud, and then pull it up again with a core of mud inside. The mud is pushed out carefully on to a bit of guttering, and by looking along the core they can look back in time. Each part of this core carries a record of what has come off the hills in the years when it accumulated.

Look down about 14 inches, and this mud was laid down three hundred years ago – about the time of Isaac Newton. Go down 22 inches, and we're going back a thousand

years – the Battle of Hastings. A yard down, and it's almost three thousand years ago. Five yards down, and we're looking at the sediments of about fifteen thousand years ago, accumulated from the melting glaciers.

There are two clear discontinuities in the Windermere cores. There's a sharp change from pink mud to brown, which corresponds to the period when the glaciers finally disappeared from the Lake District some ten thousand years ago, and open tundra landscape gave way to trees and shrubs; after that there is more organic sediment, containing well-preserved remains of plants and animals. Then, towards the top of the sedimentary record, there is a rapid darkening, where the mud goes from brown to black. This happened between AD 1820 and 1850, when railways brought people into the area in ever larger numbers, and they began to pollute the lake with their sewage. But

John Mackereth.

The Mackereth bottom corer breaks the surface of Lake Windermere.

The Mackereth corer is retrieved from another mission. Powered by compressed air, the large 'dustbin' first sucks the corer on to the bottom of the lake, and then lifts the filled corer to the surface.

the lake has masses of other information locked away in its mud – the radioactive fallout from the nuclear weapons tests with a peak in 1963, for example, and from the Chernobyl explosion of 1986; both now used as markers to help date mud samples.

Over the decades many devices have been used to take core samples from lake beds, but one of the most spectacular and useful is the pneumatic corer invented by Frederic John Haines Mackereth. Born in Ambleside on 22 September 1921, he was educated at Windermere Grammar School. After gaining a chemistry degree from Manchester University he spent a year in the Antarctic on a Norwegian whaler, but soon after the war he was back on the banks of Windermere.

One of the first things Mackereth did when he joined the staff of the Freshwater Biological Association (now the Institute of Freshwater Ecology) was to invent an instrument for measuring the concentration of oxygen in water. His gadget became the 'Dissolved Oxygen Meter', which is now the primary instrument that scientists use when they want to check the quality of water and the level of pollution. However, his most dramatic invention was the corer, designed in the late 1950s. The beauty of Mackereth's corer is that it needs little human effort, yet is able to collect an unbroken core 5 or 6 yards long and is light enough to be portable; so it can be taken to any lake where you can get a boat.

The corer is operated entirely by

compressed air. The instrument is lowered to the bottom, and an air-lift pump used to pull the water out of the dustbin-like chamber, which forces it into the mud and clamps it to the lake bed. Then compressed air is pumped into the outer tube, forcing the inner tube over a fixed piston and down into the mud. When it reaches the end of its travel the air fills the chamber; the excess pressure lifts the seal off the bottom, and because the whole outer case is now buoyant with air it leaps out of the water like a huge salmon, and lands with a splash, the core safe inside the inner tube (which is in fact a piece of drainpipe). Then the corer can be towed back to land and the core pushed out of the tube for examination.

Only in recent decades have people realised what damage human beings can do to even the largest lakes. Even the land clearances of the earliest settlers enriched the lakes with woodland soil erosion; since then all sorts of sewage, fertilisers and other chemicals have been dumped in the lake. John Mackereth showed that lake sediment reflects the state of local soils, which were considerably enriched by all the minerals ground up by the glaciers. Mackereth also showed that magnetic particles in the lake mud can be measured, and line up with the Earth's magnetic field. Because the magnetic poles are always wandering around the true poles, the magnetism can be used to

The history of the Lakes is revealed by mud cores like this.

provide a check on the dates of the various layers.

So a big lake like Windermere provides scientists with a wonderfully sensitive instrument that both measures and records ecological history. And the best machine for collecting mud cores from deep lakes is the pneumatic corer invented by John Mackereth.

The Freshwater Biological Association is still at Ferry House, at the western end of the ferry-crossing from Ambleside.

31. WEIGHING THE WORLD I: NEVIL MASKELYNE, AND THE ATTRACTION OF MOUNTAINS

For thousands of years philosophers had wondered about the size of the world we live on. At about the end of the seventeenth century the radius of the Earth was calculated fairly accurately; it turned out to be about 8,000 miles or 13,000 kilometres – in strikingly good agreement with the size calculated by the Greek scientist, Eratosthenes, two thousand years earlier! The next question was, how massive is it?, or in other words, what is the density of the Earth? Is it made of the same sort of rocks all the way through, or does it, as some people suggested, have a hollow core? The first person to measure the mass of the Earth was Nevil Maskelyne, and his method was based on Newton's idea of the Attraction of Mountains.

Nevil Maskelyne, Astronomer Royal and reluctant mountaineer.

In his famous book *Principia* of 1687 Newton said that if his law of gravitation was right, then on level ground a plumb-bob would hang straight down, vertically, because it would be pulled towards the centre of the Earth. However, if there was a mountain nearby, it would hang slightly sideways, because it would be attracted by the mountain as well as by the Earth. This idea came to be called the Attraction of Mountains. Most people thought the Attraction of Mountains was just a nuisance, because it prevented them from measuring an accurate vertical in mountainous places, but in 1772 the Astronomer Royal, Nevil Maskelyne, had a clever idea, which was to use the Attraction of Mountains to do two things – first to check Newton's prediction about the Law of Gravitation, and secondly, to weigh the world – or, more accurately, to measure the mass of the Earth.

Nevil Maskelyne was born on 6 October 1732, went to Westminster School and Trinity College, Cambridge, and became an astronomer after seeing an eclipse of the sun when he was sixteen. He was highly successful; he was sent to observe the Transit of Venus from St Helena in 1761, and he became Astronomer Royal in 1765. He suggested to the Royal Society the idea of an experiment to measure the mass of the Earth, and they were full of enthusiasm.

Charles Mason had just come back from surveying the Mason–Dixon line in America – this was the boundary between Maryland and Pennsylvania, or in other words it separated the land of slavery from the land of the free. Mason was sent off, at half a guinea a day plus expenses, to tour the highlands of Scotland on

The very attractive Schiehallion.

[500]

XLIX. *An Account of Obſervations made on the Mountain* Schehallien *for finding its Attraction. By the Rev.* Nevil Maſkelyne, *B. D. F. R. S. and Aſtronomer Royal.*

Redde, July 6, 1775.

IN the year 1772, I preſented the foregoing propoſal, for meaſuring the attraction of ſome hill in this kingdom by aſtronomical obſervations, to the Royal Society; who, ever inclined to promote uſeful obſervations which may enlarge our views of nature, honoured it with their approbation. A committee was in conſequence appointed, of which number I was one, to conſider of a proper hill whereon to try the experiment, and to prepare every thing neceſſary for carrying the deſign into execution. The Society was already provided with a ten-feet zenith ſector made by Mr. SISSON, furniſhed with an achromatic object glaſs, the principal inſtrument requiſite for this experiment, the ſame which I took with me to St. Helena in the year 1761; which wanted nothing to make it an excellent inſtrument but to have the plumb-line made adjuſtable, ſo as to paſs before and biſect a fine point at the centre of the inſtrument. This was ordered to be done, and a new wooden ſtand provided for it, capable of procuring a motion of the ſector about a vertical axis, by means of which it could be more eaſily brought into the plane of the meridian,

[501]

ridian, or turned half round for repeating the obſervations with the plane of the inſtrument placed the contrary way, in order to find the error of the line of collimation. A large parallelopiped tent, 15½ feet ſquare and 17 feet high, was alſo provided for ſheltering both the inſtrument and the obſerver who ſhould uſe it, compoſed of joices of wood well framed together, and covered with painted canvas. The Society was likewiſe poſſeſſed of moſt of the other inſtruments requiſite for this experiment; as an aſtronomical quadrant and tranſit inſtrument made by Mr. BIRD, and an aſtronomical clock by SHELTON, which had all been provided on occaſion of the obſervations of the tranſit of Venus in 1761 or 1769. A theodolite of the beſt ſort was wanting, a neceſſary inſtrument for obtaining the figure and dimenſions of the hill. One of Mr. RAMSDEN's conſtruction of 9 inches diameter, was thought the fitteſt for the purpoſe, on account of the excellence of the plan on which it was made, and the number of its adjuſtments, being capable of meaſuring angles for the moſt part to the exactneſs of a ſingle minute. The other inſtruments prepared for this buſineſs were, two barometers of M. DE LUC's conſtruction, made by Mr. NAIRNE; a common Gunter's chain; a roll of painted tape three poles long, having feet and inches marked upon it; two fir poles of 20 feet each, and four wooden ſtands, for ſupporting them when uſed in meaſuring the baſes, and a braſs ſtandard of five feet for adjuſting them. The poles and ſtands were provided on the ſpot.

Although

Maskelyne's report of the expedition to measure the attraction of Schiehallion, and to weigh the world.

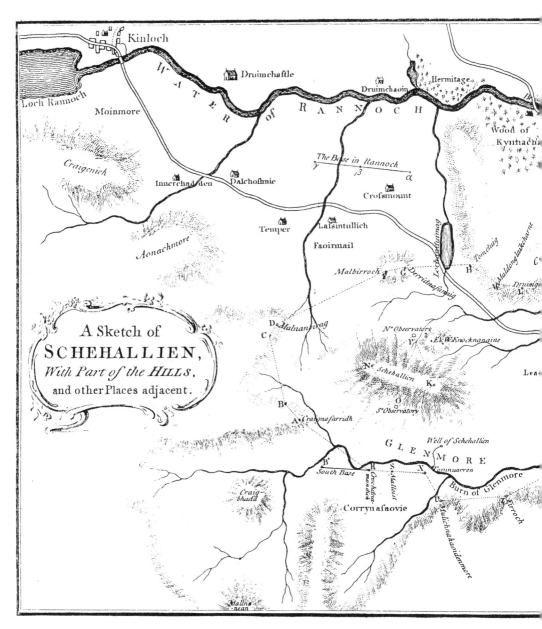

Maskelyne's map of Schiehallion, showing the north and south observatories. Note the absence of contour lines (*see* page 116).

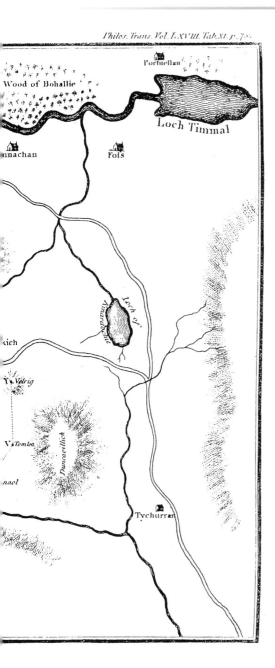

Philos. Trans. Vol. LXVIII. Tab.XI. p. 78.

horseback to find a suitable mountain. After a long journey he recommended one north of Perth, which the lowlanders called Maiden-pap, but the locals called Schiehallion. It was large and symmetrical, and there were no other mountains close by; so the plumb-bob would be attracted only by Schiehallion.

The Royal Society then asked Mason to carry out the experiment itself, but even though they offered to double his pay to a guinea a day, he refused; perhaps he'd had enough of the highland weather. So the Royal Society went back to Maskelyne, and asked him to do it. He was not keen – he certainly didn't feel the Attraction of Mountains – and said he couldn't possibly go without permission from the King, but unfortunately the King said 'Go ahead.' So reluctantly he sent his assistant ahead with all the gear, and then followed, by ship from the Thames to the Tay, and about 45 miles on horseback into the mountains. At the end of June 1774 he reached Schiehallion.

First Maskelyne set up an observatory on the south slopes of the mountain. He had a 17-foot high parallelepiped tent of painted canvas that he had found in the basement of the Royal Society. Here he set up his equipment – a 'zenith sector' – basically a telescope fixed in the north–south plane, and a plumb-bob. He had plenty of time to get organised. The weather was so bad that three weeks went by before he could make a single observation, but finally, on 20 July, he was able to begin. His plan was to observe a number of chosen stars as each one crossed the meridian. So he lay on the ground, lined up his telescope precisely on each star in turn, and measured how far it was from the 'vertical' as shown by the plumb-bob. Because the plumb-bob was attracted by the mountain the angles were all slightly 'wrong', so he expected his observations to suggest he was a bit further south than his true position.

After six weeks he shifted camp to the north slopes of the mountain – the move took twelve men a week! – set up his bothy and observatory, and observed the same stars again. This time he expected the observations to suggest he was further north than he really was. From his observations, he knew he could work out the apparent difference in latitude between the two observatories – in other words, how far the northern one seemed to be north of the southern one. Meanwhile a team of surveyors had been squelching round through the heather with theodolites and chains, working out how far apart the observatories actually were, and also the exact shape and volume of the mountain.

Nevil Maskelyne spent four months on Schiehallion, and made 337 observations of forty-three different stars. When he finished his work, at the end of October, he held a party in his bothy both to celebrate and to thank the surveyors and the locals who had helped. It must have been quite a party, for a keg of whisky was consumed; the bothy caught fire, and the local fiddler's violin was burned; Maskelyne sent him another from London.

On 6 July 1775 Maskelyne presented the Royal Society with the results. The real difference in latitude of the two observatories was almost exactly 1 mile; but from his observations he had calculated the distance to be 1 mile 480

yards. So there was a discrepancy of 480 yards. In other words, by the tiniest amount, the plumb-bob had indeed felt the attraction of the mountain. So Newton had been right – his theory of gravitation was confirmed – and Maskelyne was awarded the Copley Medal for his heroic experiment.

But what did his result tell them about the Earth? To work out the answer they hired a mathematician called Charles Hutton (*see* page 116). Hutton's calculations gave a value for the density of the Earth of 4.5 grams per cubic centimetre, and the mass of the Earth as about 5×10^{21} tonnes – that is five thousand million million million tonnes. In fact Newton had guessed a slightly more accurate value, and we now reckon it has a density of about 5.5 g/cm^3, and a mass of 6.6×10^{21} tonnes. However, Maskelyne's was the first measurement of the mass of the Earth; it was within about 20 per cent; and twenty years were to go by before anyone did it better. What's more, because relative masses had already been calculated, this single measured figure allowed Maskelyne and Hutton to work out the masses of the Moon, the Sun, and all the other planets in the solar system!

And the result did clear up one major dispute. Many people thought the Earth was hollow, but Maskelyne and Hutton utterly disproved that – indeed they suggested the Earth's core was very dense, and might even be made of metal. This was a triumph for the application of pure science and the Attraction of Mountains.

Schiehallion is south-west of Tummel Bridge – GR 272754; a plaque by the picnic area on the small road north-east of the mountain describes the great event.

32. WEIGHING THE WORLD II: JOHN MICHELL, AND BLACK HOLES

In the latter part of the eighteenth century the centre of scientific debate in the north of England was the Rectory at Thornhill, near Dewsbury in Yorkshire. The rector was the remarkable John Michell, who at the age of thirty-seven had retired from being Professor of Geology at Cambridge, where he also lectured on arithmetic, geometry, theology, philosophy, Hebrew and Greek. He used to hold entertainments for such friends as Joseph Priestley, discoverer of oxygen, John Smeaton, the engineer, Henry Cavendish, the silent physicist, and itinerant German musician, William Herschel, to whom he gave his telescope; Herschel went on to become a great astronomer.

Most people think black holes were invented by Stephen Hawking, or Albert Einstein. Not so. In 1783 Michell wrote to the Royal Society imagining a heavenly body five hundred times more massive than the Sun. An object falling towards it, he said, would eventually fall faster than light. In other words even light could not escape. John Michell was describing the black hole.

Towards the end of his life he devised a clever way of measuring the mass of the Earth. He fixed a small lead ball on each end of a long horizontal rod, and suspended it by a fine wire at the centre. Then he brought up two large lead balls,

> 42   Mr. MICHELL *on the Means of discovering the*
>
>   16. Hence, according to article 10, if the semi-diameter of a sphære of the same density with the sun were to exceed that of the sun in the proportion of 500 to 1, a body falling from an infinite height towards it, would have acquired at its surface a greater velocity than that of light, and consequently, supposing light to be attracted by the same force in proportion to its vis inertiæ, with other bodies, all light emitted from such a body would be made to return towards it, by its own proper gravity.
>
>   17. But if the semi-diameter of a sphære, of the same density with the sun, was of any other size less than 497 times that of the sun, though the velocity of the light emitted from

The paragraph in Michell's 1783 Phil. Trans. paper describing the idea of a black hole.

so that one was beside each of the small ones. Newton's law of gravitation meant the small balls would be attracted microscopically sideways by the large ones, so the rod would swing slightly clockwise from its normal rest position. Then he moved the large balls round to the other side of the small ones, so that the rod would swing anticlockwise. From the twist of the wire he could measure the gravitational force exerted on the small balls by the large ones, and from that he could work out the relative masses of the lead balls and the Earth. Unfortunately he died before carrying out the experiment, but he left the apparatus to his friend Henry Cavendish, who in 1798 measured the mass of the Earth at six thousand million million million tonnes – essentially the accepted value today. The unfair twist in the tale is that this is now called Cavendish's experiment.

The old rectory at Thornhill, near Dewsbury, is across the road from the Church of St Michael and All Angels.

33. AND THE EARTH MOVED: JOHN 'EARTHQUAKE' MILNE

In 1974 the Japanese ambassador to Great Britain made a pilgrimage to a tiny, rather nondescript village on the Isle of Wight. On a grassy bank he planted a cherry tree in memory of a local resident. This man, better known in Japan than in Britain, made the village of Shide the world centre for seismology. He was known as John 'Earthquake' Milne (1850–1913).

John Milne was born in Liverpool in 1850. At thirteen, he won a trip to the Lake District, and was so struck by the beautiful hills that he ran away to Ireland to see the scenery there. However, he soon buckled down to a career in geology, studying at the Royal School of Mines. He clearly had a taste for adventure, and despite his parents' misgivings undertook a dangerous expedition to Iceland in 1871. Having caught the

John 'Earthquake' Milne.

exploration bug, he went to Newfoundland and Arabia, before his career really took off.

In 1875 Milne was offered the post of Professor of Geology and Mining at the Imperial College of Engineering, Tokyo. This was good news and bad: despite his adventurous streak, Milne got terribly seasick, and had to travel to Tokyo overland, through a Siberian winter. In 1875 there wasn't a railway, and he had to travel by carriage, boat, sleigh and even camel. On the night he arrived, there was an earthquake, and although his first job was to catalogue Japanese volcanoes, earthquakes really fascinated him.

Milne had two great achievements. First, he founded the scientific study of earthquakes (he is known as the 'father of modern seismology'). Secondly, he invented the instrument that made it possible, the horizontal pendulum seismograph. Milne's primary aim was to record how the earth moves in earthquakes. There were two rather obvious problems. You didn't know when, or where, the earthquake would occur. The first problem could be easily but tediously solved by recording earth movements all the time, just in case an earthquake happens. The second had proved insoluble: unless you are lucky enough to be near the epicentre of the earthquake, there are no discernible earth movements. Milne realised that in fact an earthquake would cause a disturbance at a distance, possibly all round the world, but that in most places the earthquake waves would be drowned by local effects, such as people walking about in the next room. However, he had defined the problem. It would be possible to detect earthquakes at a distance if there was something characteristic about earthquake waves that let you separate them from the bigger local disturbances.

Although the Chinese had used

Milne's earthquake observatory at Shide was visited by all sorts of people. Joining Tone (centre) and Milne (second left) is Robert Falcon Scott – 'Scott of the Antarctic' (far left).

seismoscopes as long ago as AD 132, the first real seismometer was made by J.D. Forbes at Comrie in Perthshire in 1841, using an inverted pendulum. Milne also used a pendulum, but realised that earthquake waves would show up as sideways movements, so his was a horizontal pendulum. Essentially a pivoted arm with a weight on the end, suspended by a wire, he found that he could tune the seismometer by adjusting the length of pendulum arm, the size of weight and the tension in the wire. This brilliant device was able to pick up the characteristic earthquake waves, even when there were much bigger local vibrations. He made it into a seismograph, capable of continuously recording earthquakes, by attaching a pen to the end of the arm. Milne is a hero in Japan both because he put the study of earthquakes on a scientific footing, and because his understanding of earthquake

waves allowed him to make the first serious suggestions about how earthquake damage to buildings could be prevented.

On 17 February 1895 Milne's house and observatory in Tokyo were destroyed by fire. He returned to England, setting up a new earthquake observatory at Shide Hill House. He caused something of a stir locally when he arrived with his Japanese wife Tone and assistant Mr Hirota. Reports flooded in from all over the world, and a steady flow of visitors came to see John and Tone, including Robert Falcon Scott – Scott of the Antarctic. The only visitors not welcome were members of the press, who camped on the door step whenever any large earthquake had been detected.

In contrast to his importance in Japan, in Britain he was virtually ignored by the authorities. The Post Office refused to supply him with a time signal (synchronisation of signals being vital to accurate measurement).

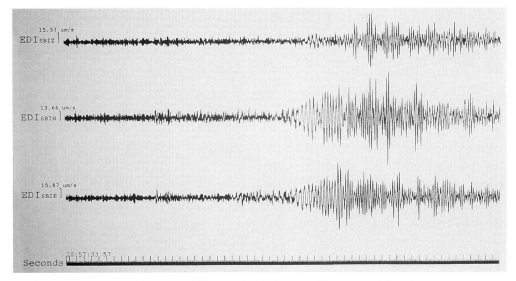

Milne's seismograph meant that this trace of the 1995 Kobe earthquake in Japan could be recorded in Edinburgh.

Eventually, in 1900 the Eiffel tower began to broadcast time signals, and a Mr Shaw set up a crystal receiver for Milne with an aerial between two elm trees.

In Shide, Milne was able to detect earthquakes so clearly that it became the world centre for seismology. To correct for local effects, he established a second instrument on the Island at Carisbrooke Castle. Another series of experiments was undertaken at Ryde, to try to establish the tilting of the seabed at high tide. Every week the trace showed huge swings,

How the earth moved for John 'Earthquake' Milne.

which confused Milne. Eventually he discovered that the signals did in a way record the earth moving since they coincided with times when the butler and the housekeeper were off duty at the same time. He further claimed that from the traces taken at Shide he could tell how long the gravel trucks were stationary at the Barley Mow pub.

Shide Hill House is not as it was in Milne's day. Much has been demolished or rebuilt, and a new extension obscures the outside of the great observatory. However, there is one relic of Milne. Inside the house, in what is now a spare bedroom, a plaque has been found under the wallpaper. Originally on the outside of the house, it reads 'Earthquake Observatory 1900', the only clue that this was once a world-class laboratory. After Milne's death in June 1913, the station was kept running for six years, but then the house was sold and Tone returned to Japan.

John Milne's home and laboratory are now part of a private home in Shide, but across the road, by the river, is the cherry tree planted in his honour by the Japanese ambassador.

34. SCIENCE ON THE ROCKS: THE SCORESBYS, WHALING SCIENTISTS OF WHITBY

The *Dictionary of National Biography* entry for William Scoresby Jnr lists under 'Education' *The Resolution* whaler and Queen's College, Cambridge. His father, William Snr, was educated at the village school, Cropton, and on a ship called the *Jane*, trading between Whitby and the Baltic. These entries hint at the amazing lives of these father-and-son scientists, who spanned all levels of society, as well as the most dangerous parts of the globe.

William Scoresby Snr (1760–1829), son of a farmer, was born in the village of Cropton, 20 miles from Whitby. He first worked on the farm at the age of nine, and did not go to sea until he was twenty, when he became an apprentice on the *Jane*. William was a superb navigator, and in his second year at sea he detected a navigational error which might have resulted in the loss of the ship. Far from being grateful, the mate (whose fault it was) became so unpleasant that Scoresby left the ship in 1781 and joined the *Speedwell*, carrying stores to Gibraltar. It was not a happy voyage: in the Straits of Gibraltar they were captured by the Spanish, and thrown into jail. Scoresby and a friend managed to escape, and made their way home, where Scoresby embarked on his career with the Greenland whaling fleet.

It must have been an extraordinary life. Scoresby never saw a summer in Whitby, always preferring to make the profitable voyage north. He became the most successful whaler ever, taking record catches and making the most profit, totalling £90,000 in thirty years at sea. He also held the record for the highest latitude ever attained by a ship. He was a bit of an inventor, his most famous creation being the 'crow's nest', a barrel hoisted into the rigging to provide some protection for the look-out against the Arctic winds.

Against this background, it is not surprising that William Scoresby Jnr (1789–1857) worshipped his father, and wanted to follow in his footsteps. When he was just ten, William went aboard his father's ship to say goodbye before that summer's voyage to Greenland. When it was time to return ashore, William hid his hat, hoping the delay would result in his being left on board. His father gave in, and the pilots went

William Scoresby.

William Scoresby snr, world-record whaler and inventor of the crow's nest.

William Scoresby Jnr was a gifted artist, recording Arctic wildlife and the perils of whaling.

Assistance was not very distant and after a few minutes in hazard of perishing we were happily rescued without having sustained any particular injury.'

William not only tolerated the hard life, he positively cultivated it. Having entered Edinburgh University in 1806, the same year he accompanied his father on the latitude record-breaking voyage, he volunteered for the navy, wanting to experience the life of an ordinary seaman. When he left the navy, he had a bit of luck. Returning home from Portsmouth he met Sir Joseph Banks, the famous botanist on Cook's first voyage. Banks was by then President of the Royal Society – top man in British science – a post he held for forty years until his death in 1820. Banks took Scoresby to a few social gatherings in London, and introduced him to the scientific elite. Perhaps Banks exhibited the brave and muscular whaler as a bit of exotica from the north, but whatever the reason, they became friends and corresponded until Banks's death. Banks suggested to Scoresby that he should start recording the natural phenomena he observed on his voyages, since really good scientific records of the Arctic were rare.

Scoresby turned out to be an excellent natural scientist, not least because of his skill as an artist. His drawings and paintings were superb, often recording dramatic whaling incidents, as well as animals and plants never seen by Europeans. Scoresby was much more than a keen observer, and he began to build up an impressive list of scientific theories and discoveries. He was the first person to suggest that the peculiar colours of the Arctic seas were due to

William Scoresby jnr, Arctic scientist.

ashore, leaving young William to begin his great career at sea. He became a captain in his own right when he was twenty-one years old.

Scoresby's journal records a particularly dramatic incident. Chasing after one whale, the other boats couldn't keep up. But Scoresby had noticed that the whale kept to a circular path, and positioned his boat where he expected it to surface. But he was almost too clever for his own good: '. . . having marked the proceedings of the fish, I selected a situation where I conceived it was likely to make its appearance. It arose in the very spot, and though unperceived by us struck the boat such a blow the bottom was driven in, a hole fifteen square feet in area, and the boat sank in a moment.

what he called 'minute animalcules', what we would call plankton. Using a microscope, he was the first to record the beautiful shapes of snowflakes – a task made easier, it is true, by working in sub-zero temperatures where the snowflakes do not melt!

He found a surprising result from his 'Marine Diver'. The Diver was a box containing a thermometer that was lowered into the ocean, and could record the temperature at various depths. He discovered that in the Arctic ocean, the deeper you go, the warmer it gets, which confounded previous ideas.

Perhaps his most spectacular work was on magnetism. He discovered that if you hammer a piece of soft iron, it becomes a weak magnet – if you line it up with the earth's magnetic field. Stuck in the ice in Greenland one summer, he found that if he hammered a second piece of iron with the first, the magnet got stronger, and so he built up what is known as the Greenland Magnet. This is now in the museum at Whitby, together with his drawings and specimens, and still lifts a 10 lb weight

with ease. Scoresby reckoned that a man lost at sea could quickly construct a compass to navigate home, should he happen to have soft iron nail and a hammer about his person.

Scoresby clearly had the respect of his men. One of his favourite tricks was to mould a lens from ice using the warmth of his hands, and use it to light the sailors' pipes – fire from ice. He became a very moral person, and in particular believed the Sabbath should be respected. Once he entertained a couple of rough whaling captains to Sunday breakfast, and although he prayed fervently following the stream of blasphemy he had witnessed, he caught hardly any whales the following week, and resolved always to be pious on Sundays. He eventually left the sea to become a vicar, and preached in 1826 at St Mary's Church to a congregation mourning the loss in storms of the *Lively* and the *Esk* – the last two whaling ships to sail from Whitby.

The Whitby Museum in Pannett Park, open most days (01947 602908), has a replica of William snr's crow's nest, and many beautiful original drawings and paintings by William jnr, as well as the huge magnet he made while stuck in the ice off Greenland.

35. HOW IT ALL STACKS UP: WILLIAM SMITH'S GEOLOGICAL MAP OF BRITAIN

Two hundred years ago, most people believed the earth was only six thousand years old, and had been created exactly in the way the Bible says. But a man who lived and worked in Scarborough, who had hardly any education, changed all that. Just by looking at the rocks, he worked out the structure not just of Scarborough but of the whole of England and Wales. This amazing one-man feat almost bankrupted him, but William Smith became known as the Father of English Geology.

William Smith was born in Oxfordshire in 1769, the eldest of three children. His family had been yeoman farmers and William was educated at the village school, which was all the education a boy of that background could expect. Even as a boy he collected fossils. His uncle apparently lent him some books, and he taught himself basic geometry: this was enough to get him a job helping Edward Webb, a land surveyor. Webb was an inspiring teacher, and Smith was soon expert in recognising the underlying soils and rocks of Oxfordshire. However, the picture of the layers of rock that emerged was confusing, and most people thought that each area had its own arrangement. In 1793 Smith was given his first surveying job, on a canal through the Somerset coalfield. This was a wonderful opportunity for him to examine the exposed layers of rock in a different part of the country, work he continued when he was sent on a sort of national canal tour by his employers.

Fossil-collecting had up to this time been a rather haphazard hobby. The strange rocky creatures were fascinating, but made little sense, as this was well before evolution became accepted. Smith's sharp mind and great observational skill were to change all that. Casual observers working in different locations might notice that in one place a layer of sandstone was on top of a layer of, say, shale, whereas in another place the reverse was true. Smith wanted to know if the shale was part of the same layer in each place, or a different one. But how could he do that without digging from one place to the other? By recording where he had found fossils on his travels, he began to work out a system. It made sense if he identified layers of rock *according to the fossils found in them*. By this method he could for instance say whether clay exposed in canal workings in Somerset was part of the same layer he knew in his native Oxfordshire. He amazed two amateur fossil-collectors, the Revd Townsend and the Revd Richardson, when he was able to pick up their fossils and tell them exactly what sort of rocks they had come from.

William Smith, the 'Father of English Geology'.

The Rotunda Museum, Scarborough. William Smith's circular design was meant to concentrate the mind of the visitor on the layers in the rock.

Because he had travelled so extensively, he began to build up a picture of the layers of rock across the whole country, realising that they were stacked up in a regular order. He also came to an obvious but controversial conclusion – that the oldest rocks must be at the bottom, and the youngest at the top. He earned the nickname 'Strata Smith' and in 1815 he was finally able to publish the first ever geological map of England and Wales, showing the structure of the land. But the project almost bankrupted him, and he had to sell his London home in 1819. According to his nephew, he had 'scarcely any home but the rocks'. He stayed wherever he was professionally engaged, eventually moving to Yorkshire and, finally, to Scarborough. Although he seemed happy in the town, and fell in with the local worthies, he never recovered financially from making his great map, for which he had been paid just £50.

Scarborough was rather late in having a Philosophical Society: the annual report for 1830 says that the previous 'formation of societies in York, Hull, Leeds and Whitby . . . were enough to raise a blush in the cheek of every inhabitant who was a true lover of nature and a friend of the propagation of science'. Once the society was formed, it needed a museum, and Smith had a brilliant idea. He suggested that the museum should be made entirely circular. Rock and fossil specimens could be set out on sloping shelves round the circular interior, arranged correctly in order of the strata in which they were found. In this way, Smith hoped, the public would come to look on the display not merely as a collection of individual pieces, but as a representation of the way the rocks of the country are organised. Although Smith's collection of rocks was sold long ago, the elegant Rotunda still stands, beneath the Grand Hotel, on the sea front at Scarborough, a wonderful expression of the

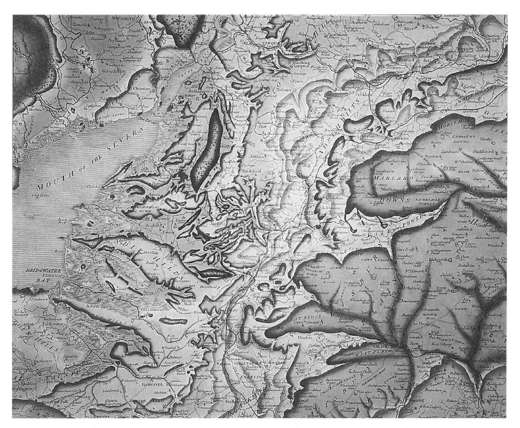

Part of Smith's geological map of Britain, completed in 1815. This magnificent solo effort virtually bankrupted him, and he never really recovered.

ideas of William Smith. Around the inside of the dome is a cross-section of the Yorkshire coast, painted by William Smith's nephew, John Phillips, who became one of the most important geologists of his day and a founder of the British Association.

Far from retiring in comfort and glory, Smith fell on hard times. Unlike the vicars and doctors of the Philosophical Society, Smith was a working man with nowhere to live. Luckily the president of the Philosophical Society, Sir John Johnstone, took pity on him and offered him the job of land steward on his estate at Hackness, a few miles west of Scarborough. Smith felt secure but trapped at Hackness, and the only geological work he did there was a map of the estate. Eventually, he won some recognition. In February 1831 the council of the Geological Society voted him the Wollaston medal. This was the first time it was awarded, and was so new that the medal had not actually been struck yet, and had to be presented the following year. He resigned from Hackness, and his supporters were able to get him a pension of £100. But it was scarcely enough, and at the end of his life Smith, whose mind was as active as ever, was unable to take part in the great science he had helped to establish.

The layers are clearly visible in Castle Cliff, Scarborough. At the Rotunda Museum in Museum Terrace, Vernon Road, there is a bust of Smith and a wonderful geological cross-section of the Yorkshire coast, painted by his nephew.

36. FOSSIL-FINDER MARY ANNING

In the centre of Lyme Bay lies the attractive town of Lyme Regis, its tiny harbour protected by the great curving rock wall known as the Cobb, made famous in Jane Austen's *Persuasion* and John Fowles's *The French Lieutenant's Woman*. For hundreds of years Lyme Regis has been famous for what used to be called 'curiosities'. We know them as fossils, and they are found in the Blue Lias in the cliffs on either side of the town. Walk along the beach and you can see how the cliffs are gradually eroding and tumbling into the sea. Each time a slab falls off it brings with it nodules of grey rock containing fossils – the remnants of the rich life in the warm muddy sea that swirled there two hundred million years

If Mary Anning had been a man, would she be famous?

ago. Fossil-hunters are out in force each time the tide goes out, especially when the cliffs are washed down with heavy rain. They seek out new nodules and crack them open with hammers, looking for the fossils that may lie within.

Mary Anning was born in Lyme Regis in 1799. At the age of fifteen months she survived a lightning strike which killed the three women she was with. Family legend has it that she had been a dull child before, but after this accident she became lively and intelligent, and grew up so. Mary's father Richard was a carpenter, but he used to supplement his income by selling curiosities, and following his death when she was twelve, Mary did the same. But if fossils had been a side-line for Richard, they became Mary's life, and she became the greatest fossil-hunter of the age. She was poor, and had little formal education; yet she helped to bring about one of the truly great scientific revolutions, which overturned our view of the history of the world and the origins of life.

Her astonishing success began one day in 1811, the year after her father's death, when Mary and her brother Joseph were looking for curiosities somewhere under Black Ven, the hill half a mile east of the town. Scraping around in the muddy rock, they found the skull of what looked like a crocodile. The following year Mary returned and extracted the body – an amazing feat, because the creature was 30 feet long and entirely encased in rock! In fact she had to hire a gang of men to help her. The skeleton turned out to be not a crocodile, but one of the finest specimens of the recently discovered icthyosaurus.

The icthyosaurus was sold for £23, a tidy sum for a very poor family, and

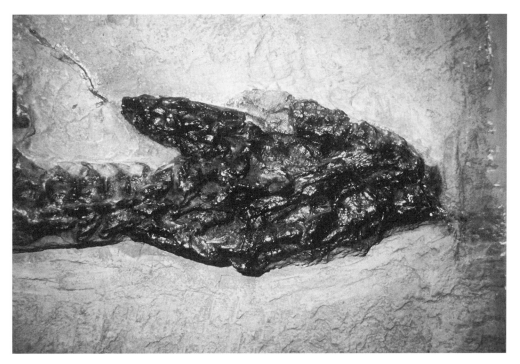

Head of *Plesiosaurus* from the lower Jurassic, Lyme Regis. This was the first articulated plesiosaur ever found, and one of Mary Anning's greatest disoveries.

Mary's mother encouraged the girl to look for other specimens. In 1823 she found the first ever plesiosaur fossil, and in 1828 the first pterodactyl. In the intervening years, she found several examples of each, in addition to coprolites, a cephalopod and a fossil fish called *Squaloraja*. All of these she extracted, prepared and reassembled with incredible skill. Lady Silvester wrote on 17 September 1824: 'The extraordinary thing in this young woman is that she has made herself so thoroughly acquainted with the science that the moment she finds any bones she knows to what tribe they belong.'

The Philpot Museum stands above the sea at the very centre of Lyme Regis, where the road, after plunging down the hill, turns sharply back up the other side.

It was named after a family Mary knew; the three Philpot daughters were well-known fossil collectors, and may have inspired her in her work. However, they were young ladies; Mary lived a very different life. The house where she lived and worked was on the same site – it was pulled down to make room for the museum. Outside was a table where she showed off and sold her latest specimens, and down below was the basement workshop where Mary brought the raw specimens from the cliff to be 'developed'.

Developing a specimen means separating it from the surrounding rock – fantastically delicate work, especially with an unknown species where you don't know what it is supposed to look like. Mary was a brilliant developer. She also

Mary Anning's house at Lyme Regis. Her workshop was in the cellar, and she sold fossils from a round table in front of the house.

understood anatomy enough to get her specimens assembled correctly, and of course she had the amazing ability to find them in the first place. A poem was written about her in 1884:

Miss Anning, as a child, ne'er passed
A pin upon the ground
But picked it up; and so at last
An icthyosaurus found.

Mary Anning was born in the right place at the right time. Philosophers were just beginning to think about what fossils meant. Until that time they were regarded simply as curiosities, because they didn't fit into the history of the world as portrayed in the Bible. The Earth was supposed to be only a few thousand years old, and the fossils were reckoned by many to have been in the rocks from the start – perhaps put there by God as a test of faith.

Mary Anning's skill meant that fossils of real scientific value were available to scientists like William Buckland (*see* opposite), who were formulating a new history of the earth that led eventually to the idea of evolution. Mary was well known to scientists and fossil-collectors. Some said she became a little arrogant, and she seems to have been a tough, slightly difficult character. Anna Maria Pinney wrote in her journal on 25 October 1831: 'Went out at 11 o'clock fossilising with Mary Anning . . . She has been noticed by all the cleverest men in England, who have her to stay at their houses, correspond with her on geology etc. This has completely turned her head, and she has the proudest and most unyielding spirit I have ever met with . . . She glories in being afraid of no one and in saying everything she pleases.'

But if she was temporarily famous, she certainly wasn't rich; the family still teetered on the brink of poverty. On one occasion they hadn't had a really good fossil find for over a year, and were selling their furniture to pay the rent; a kind collector sold his collection to save them. Mary's specimens were all sold to collectors, but when they ended up in museums they bore the names of the men who had bought them, rather than the woman who had discovered them.

If Mary Anning had been an educated man, and so able to publish her own scientific papers, she might now be seriously famous. How unfair that most people have never heard of the carpenter's teenage daughter who helped to unravel the history of life on earth.

The Philpot Museum in Lyme Regis, on the site of Mary Anning's house, has a collection of memorabilia.

37. WILLIAM BUCKLAND, AND HYENA BONES IN YORKSHIRE

In 1820 workmen repairing roads in Kirkdale, North Yorkshire, were surprised to find a large number of old bones mixed up with the rocks they were taking from the quarry. At first they thought the bones must have belonged to cows that had fallen in, although there seemed to be more of these bones in the cave beside the quarry, known as Kirkdale Cavern.

When the news of the bones spread, collectors turned up in droves to add to their cabinets of curiosities. A local vicar sent some to his friend the Bishop of Oxford, and he in turn showed them to the newly appointed Professor of Geology at the University, the Revd William Buckland. Buckland was a splendid chap. He was profoundly interested in the history of the Earth, and he believed in the dramatic. He took his Oxford students for field trips on horseback. On one memorable occasion he found a huge fossil, an ammonite. It was too large and heavy to balance on his horse, but luckily the middle

had disappeared, leaving a hole big enough to get his head and one shoulder through, so he rode home with the vast ammonite slung uncomfortably round his neck. The students laughed aloud at the sight, and dubbed him Sir Ammon, or Ammon Knight. In one of his lectures he greatly offended his stuffier colleagues by goose-stepping about the lecture theatre in order to demonstrate how prehistoric birds might have left footprints in the mud. They thought an Oxford Professor should not behave in this way, demeaning himself and turning a lecture into a circus performance. Indeed, his very appointment had stirred up controversy, for the religious enthusiasts and the scriptural geologists asserted that the Bible recorded not only the Truth, but all that was needed to be known about the distant past; so what was the point

Entrance to the Kirkdale cave.

of a Professor of Geology, other than to attack the Bible?

When Buckland heard about the bones in Kirkdale, he dropped everything and travelled at once to North Yorkshire, where in December 1821 he spent what must have been an uncomfortable week in the cave. He wrote a detailed account of what he found, which was published by the Royal Society in February 1822.

The Kirkdale Cave was a long tunnel, varying between 2 and 5 feet wide, and extending horizontally north-east for about 100 yards. In only a few places was it high enough to allow him to stand up, and although there were a few side-tunnels, there was no other exit apart from the mouth, which had been exposed by the quarrying. On the floor of the cave was a foot of mud,

and in this mud were the broken pieces of thousands of bones. The bones had come from a wide variety of animals, including giant deer, hippos, rhinos and even straight-tusked elephants. There were one or two teeth from lions and bears, and many bones from such smaller animals as rabbits and water-rats. Almost all the larger bones were broken, with jagged edges. But by far the most common bones in the cave were those of hyenas; Buckland found fragments from at least three hundred individual animals. In particular the lower jaws, with four savage molars, could not have come from any other species. The jaws in the cave were about one third larger than those of the 'modern Cape hyena', but otherwise identical.

For Buckland it was clear that the foot of mud was the residue of the Flood, but

Exploring the Kirkdale Cave.

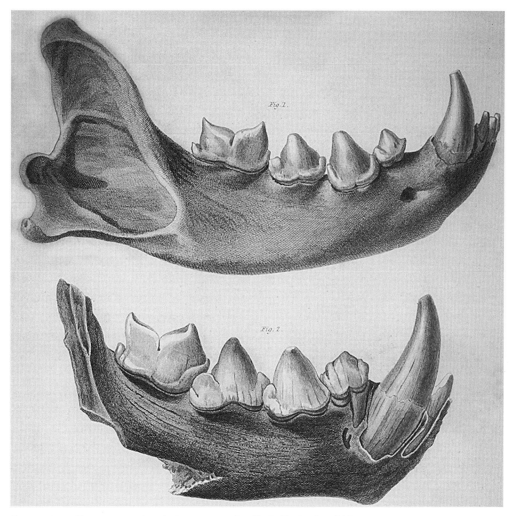

Hyena jaw bones. The top one is modern, the bottom one was found by Buckland in the Kirkdale Cave.

he was left with a real mystery; a cave in the middle of North Yorkshire full of the bones of animals normally thought to be tropical. How on earth had they got in there? There was no shortage of theories. All of them had to fit in with the 'known facts' – that the world had been created in six days in 4004 BC, and the Flood had happened only about ten generations later, as reported in the Bible.

One theory was that all these animals had been living in Yorkshire when the Flood happened. Terrified by the rising waters, they had all rushed into the cave for safety, and were drowned where they sheltered. The problem is, it's hard to believe that rabbits and deer would rush to shelter in a cave with three hundred hyenas, and anyway, as the entrance is only 2 feet high, no elephant or rhino could have squeezed in, however scared it was.

Another theory was that the waters of the Flood had been so violent that they swirled animals all around the world, and tropical animals had been swirled up from Africa to Yorkshire, where they had fallen into the cave through a hole in the roof. Unfortunately there was no hole in the roof.

Maybe, said a third theory, the Flood was so violent it smashed all the animals into pieces, which was how the big ones got in through the entrance, and why the bones were broken. But then surely they would also have been worn smooth, like the pebbles on a beach. The bones in the cave had sharp splintered ends.

Another theory suggested that the animals had indeed all lived in Yorkshire, but that food had become scarce. The hyenas had eaten all the other animals to extinction, one by one, and had then turned on one another, until there was only one left. The last hyena had eaten itself!

Although this last idea is absurd, the theory is not so far from the conclusion Buckland reached. He suggested that for hundreds or even thousands of years the cave had been a den for generations of hyenas, which had foraged for food in the neighbouring countryside. Hyenas will eat either fresh meat or carrion, and must have dragged whole carcasses or parts back into the cave, which would explain the great variety of bones. The fact that the bones were all broken would also fit in with this, for hyenas are known to crunch up their bones to reach the marrow. Buckland even found what he thought were teeth-marks on some of the bones, and to support his theory he performed a cunning experiment, of a kind that is rarely possible in either biology or palaeontology. When a travelling menagerie came to Oxford from Exeter, Buckland procured the hindquarters of an ox, and fed them to the hyena. The hyena, understandably surprised to be given lunch by the professor, performed admirably, not only crunching the ends off the bones, but even leaving tooth-marks identical to those found on the bones from the cave.

Buckland's conclusion – that the cave had been home to generations of hyenas, in a time when tropical animals lived in Yorkshire – caused a furore that rumbled on for twenty years, because he was describing life centuries before the Flood. This was dangerous ground and he was repeatedly attacked for his heretical views. The Dean of York said 'If Buckland be right, Moses must be wrong!'

The Kirkdale Cave turned out not to be unique. A similar collection of bones was found in a cave on Durdham Down near Bristol in 1842, while in Kent's Hole in Torquay William Pengelly found bones of mammoth, woolly rhinoceros, cave-bear, cave-lion and the extinct sabre-toothed tiger, but Buckland's discoveries at Kirkdale started the trouble. The split between religion and science was developing. In 1840 another geologist, Professor William Whewell, wrote that a new name was needed for those who wished to study science for its own sake; he proposed they should be called 'scientists'.

The Kirkdale Cave is near the river 1 mile west of Kirkbymoorside, though the mud and the bones have gone, and the entrance is up a precarious and muddy cliff.

MATHEMAGICIANS

Mathematics is the purest of the sciences, and the only one whose advance has not had to wait for technology. The purest of mathematical ideas come only to prepared brains; they cannot be accelerated by machines; even computers are rarely helpful in the creative philosophy of pure maths. That is one good reason why so much mathematics was sorted out by the ancient Greeks, and why the three oldest heroes in this book were all mathematicians.

38. ALCUIN, PUZZLER TO CHARLEMAGNE

The wolf, the goat and the cabbage.

Puzzle 1: You have to cross a river, taking with you a wolf, a goat and a cabbage. You have a boat, but in it you can carry only one of these at a time. The problem is that if you take the wolf, then while you are away the goat will eat the cabbage. However, if you take the cabbage, then the wolf will eat the goat! The puzzle is, how can you get them all across the river safely?

This puzzle was written down as one of a collection of 'problems to sharpen the young' by an English scholar called Flaccus Albinus Alcuinus, or Alcuin, as he is generally remembered.

Alcuin was born in York about AD 735, went to Rome in 780, became Abbot of Tours, and settled in Aachen as what would now be Minister of Education for the European Community, but was then a close adviser to Charlemagne, who became Holy Roman Emperor on Christmas Day in the year 800.

Some of Alcuin's *Propositiones ad acuendos juvenes* are fairly trivial, but among the river-crossing puzzles are some really tricky ones. Try this on your friends:

Puzzle 2: Mum and dad and two children have to cross a river. The boat will hold only one adult or two children; not even one adult and one child. How do they get across?

And if they manage that, here's a really tough one:

Puzzle 3: Three married couples have to cross a river, and for religious reasons no woman must be left with a man unless her husband is there. The boat will carry only two. How do they all cross?

What is fascinating about these puzzles is not just that they are good puzzles – they challenge the mind, they seem impossible, and then when you work one out you get a sense of achievement – but that they are 1,200 years old, and still as good as new.

The solution to Puzzle 1, in case you are still suffering, is to take the goat across, leave it, return for either the wolf or the cabbage, take it across, *bring the goat back*, take the cabbage or the wolf, and finally return for the goat.

St Peter's School, Clifton, York, claims to have been founded by Alcuin, and a college at York University, 4 miles to the south-east, is named after him.

Alcuin.

39. ROBERT RECORDE, AND THE INVENTION OF THE EQUALS SIGN

There's an age-old philosophical question, raised by Plato among many others: Was mathematics invented by people, or was it all out there in the world, waiting to be discovered? Some bits of mathematics are so familiar they seem almost to be part of nature. Take the equals sign, for example; it seems so natural you might almost expect to find one in the garden, but it was actually invented by a gentle soul and a brilliant teacher of mathematics. He introduced algebra to this country, he was the first to write about arithmetic and geometry in English, and his name was Robert Recorde.

IN MEMORY OF
ROBERT RECORDE,
THE EMINENT MATHEMATICIAN,

Robert Recorde was born in 1510. His dad was the 120th Mayor of Tenby in the south-west corner of Wales. In those days Tenby was a busy port; the harbour was surrounded by large stone houses belonging to wealthy merchants. Robert went to Oxford, became a fellow of All Souls College, and lectured on mathematics, rhetoric, music and anatomy. Later, he went to Cambridge and to London.

His first book, *The Grounde of Arts* (1543), was a simple textbook of arithmetic, but so good it went through at least fifty editions. He followed this in 1551 with *The Pathway to Knowledge*, all about geometry; *The Castle of Knowledge*, in 1556, about astronomy; and finally in 1557 *The Whetstone of Witte*. In this last book he introduced not only plus and minus signs, but the equals sign.

Apparently this sign used to be an abbreviation for *est* (which means 'is' in Latin), but he formalised it in his book: 'to avoid the tediouse repetition of these woordes: is equalle to: . . . a paire of paralleles, or gemowe [twin] lines of one lengthe, thus: $=$, bicause noe. 2. thynges can be moare equalle.'

In his first book there are 2, 3, 4, and 5 times tables, but he reckoned the later ones were too difficult; so he taught a curious method of multiplication for digits from 6 to 9, using the St Andrew's cross. Thus to multiply 7×9 he wrote 7

$$7$$
$$X$$
$$9$$

Then he subtracted both numbers from 10 and wrote in

7	3
X	
9	1

The Arte

as their workes doe extende) to diftincte it onely into twoo partes. Whereof the firfte is, *when one nomber is equalle vnto one other.* And the feconde is, *when one nomber is compared as equalle vnto 2. other nombers.*

Alwaies willyng you to remeber, that you reduce your nombers, to their leafte denominations, and fmallefte formes, before you procede any farther.

And again, if your *equation* be foche, that the greateſte denomination *Cofsike*, be ioined to any parte of a compounde nomber, you fhall tourne it fo, that the nomber of the greateſte figne alone, maie ftande as equalle to the refte.

And this is all that neadeth to be taughte, concernyng this woorke.

Howbeit, for eafie alteratiõ of *equations.* I will propounde a fewe eraples, bicaufe the extraction of their rootes, maie the more aptly bee wroughte. And to auoide the tedioufe repetition of thefe woordes : is equalle to : I will fette as I doe often in woorke vfe, a paire of paralleles, or Gemowe lines of one lengthe, thus:=======,bicaufe noe. 2. thynges, can be moare equalle. And now marke thefe nombers.

1.   14.ze.——.15.℈=====71.℈.

2.   20.ze.——.18.℈=====.102.℈.

3.   26.ʒ——10ze====9.ʒ.——10ze——213.℈.

4.   19.ze——192.℈====10ʒ——108℈——19ze

5.   18.ze——24.℈.====8.ʒ.——2.ze.

6.   34ʒ——12ze====40ze——480℈——9.ʒ

1.   In the firfte there appeareth. 2. nombers, that is 14.ze.

The page from Recorde's *The Whetstone of Witte* on which he defines the equals sign.

Multiply the right-hand digits to
give the right digit of the answer

```
      7        3
          X
      9        1
      _____
               3
```

Then subtract diagonally
(9-3 or 7-1) to give the left
digit of the answer

```
      7        3
          X
      9        1
      _____
      6        3
```

Strange, but it seems to work!

Robert Recorde died in 1558, the year that Elizabeth became Queen, and five years before William Shakespeare was born.

St Mary's Church in Tenby has a lovely memorial and portrait in relief; Tenby Museum has three original Recorde books, although not on display; open 10–4.

40. JOHN NAPIER: LOGS, BONES, AND THE DECIMAL POINT

Just as the equals sign was invented by Robert Recorde, so the decimal point was invented by another polymath, this time a Scottish aristocrat, the eighth Laird of Merchiston.

John Napier was born at Merchiston Castle in 1550. The castle is small, tall and elegant; in those days it was in remote countryside a few miles south-east of Edinburgh, but now unfortunately the castle is built into the middle of the concrete-and-glass Napier University, and the countryside is remote. John Napier, known as the 'Marvellous Merchiston', was regarded with awe. Locals said he could predict the future, and he kept a black cockerel that was supposed to be able to detect their secrets. Once, some valuables were stolen from the castle. Napier ordered his servants to go one by one into a darkened room in the tower, and there to stroke the cockerel, which he said would crow when it was touched by the

John Napier, Laird of Merchiston, astronomer and inventor of the pocket calculator.

guilty party. They all took their turns going into the room, but the cockerel remained silent. Then Napier took them into a lighted room and asked them to hold up their hands. All but one had black hands. The clean-handed servant was accused of theft; he hadn't dared touch the cockerel. In fact, Napier had covered the bird with soot.

Napier was keen on scientific agriculture; he experimented with various fertilisers on his fields. He devised a hydraulic screw for pumping water out of flooded coal pits. He also invented war machines to fend off any Spanish invasion. One was a metal chariot, propelled by those inside it, perforated with small holes from which they could fire pistols. 'The enemy', wrote Napier, 'meantime being abased and altogether uncertain what defence or pursuit to use against a moving mouth of metal.' Confused they would have been, meeting a tank in the sixteenth century.

John Napier, inventor of the first pocket calculator.

But Napier's greatest love was astronomy. The air was clear then, before Edinburgh became 'Auld Reekie', and he liked to go up to his battlements and look at the stars. However, he found all the calculations tedious, and resolved to do something about it. For twenty years he laboured, and in 1614 published his *Mirifici logarithmorum canonis descriptio*, or Description of the marvellous canon of logarithms. Log tables allowed you to multiply numbers together by simply adding. Until the days of calculators, which arrived in the 1970s, they remained the best method for doing tedious calculations. Astronomers across Europe thought the technique wonderful, and log tables were rapidly adopted.

They certainly seemed like magic to Henry Briggs. Henry was born on 23 February 1561 at Warley, near Halifax in Yorkshire. He went off to London and then to Oxford, where he became Professor of Geometry. When he first saw Napier's book, he wrote to his friend James Ussher (who later became an archbishop and calculated the date of creation as 4004 BC) and said 'Napier . . . hath set my head and hands a-work with his new and admirable logarithms. I hope to see him this summer, if it please God, for I never saw a book which pleased me better or made me more wonder.' This reaction was not shared by all the schoolchildren forced to use logs in the subsequent centuries, but then Briggs was an unusual man. He did indeed travel all the way to Merchiston, and when the butler had shown him into the presence of the Laird, they sat for fifteen minutes without a word being spoken, lost in mutual admiration!

Briggs stayed with Napier for a month in 1615, and another month in 1616. He had planned a third trip, but Napier died on 4 April 1617, before the visit could take place. Briggs made an important contribution to the use of logs. Napier had worked all his out to base e, which is about 2.718, because that is how they drop naturally out of the series used to calculate them. These are called 'natural' or 'Napierian' logarithms. But Briggs pointed out that they would be more useful if they were to base 10 instead; so he proceeded to work out thirty thousand such logs to fourteen decimal places!

For a simple example of the use of logs (to base 10), suppose you planned to order a newspaper which cost 35p every day, including weekends, and you wanted to work out how much it would cost for a year – 365 days. Look up the logs of 35 (1.54407) and 365 (2.56229) and add them together to give 4.10636; then look up the antilog, and read off the answer: 12775p, or £127.75. All you have to do is one addition, which is much easier than multiplying.

Logarithms, however, were not the end of Napier's contribution to calculations; he also invented a pocket calculator. Despite his tables, Napier still felt that arithmetic was too hard for people to learn. In his book *Rabdologiae* ('Little rods'), which also covered such neat ideas as extracting square roots by moving counters around on a chessboard, he wrote, 'Some are accustomed to make arithmetic frightening through very love of the subject. This instrument provides a readily understood explanation.' His calculator comprised a set of square-section rods with numbers written down each of the sides. They were often made of ivory, and were consequently called 'Napier's Bones'. The Bones were massively popular for more than a hundred years. When the London diarist Samuel Pepys studied arithmetic in 1667 he wrote of his tutor: 'To my chamber whither comes Jonas Moore and tells me the mighty use of Napier's Bones.'

Today we have calculators, so the Bones are less useful. But another of Napier's inventions we use every day. When he was calculating his tables, Napier had to write down fractions of a whole number, just as we write pennies as fractions of a pound. There was no really good way of writing fractions down; so Napier invented one. We still use his invention today, and it's called the decimal point.

Merchiston Castle, smartly restored, is now part of Napier University, Colinton Road, 3 miles south-east of the centre of Edinburgh.

41. NICHOLAS SAUNDERSON, BLIND MATHEMATICAL GENIUS WHO TAUGHT OTHERS TO SEE

One mile west of Penistone, high in the Yorkshire Pennines, lies the little village of Thurlstone, built dramatically on the sides of the hills, the cellar of one house being level with the roof of the three-storey house next door. Nicholas Saunderson's birth in January 1682 is commemorated by a plaque in Latin on the wall by the telephone box. When he was about a year old, Nicholas caught smallpox, and lost not merely his sight but his eyes as well. This boded ill for his future, since most of the people in the village lived by manual labour, and blind labourers were not much in demand.

However, he showed promise at the village school, and his parents sent him off to the Free Grammar School in Penistone, the seventh oldest school in the country, close to the imposing church in the centre of town. Here Nicholas found a great delight in studying the works of Isaac Newton, and turned out himself to have a gift for mathematics; but what call was there for blind mathematicians in rural Yorkshire?

In 1707 he decided to go to Cambridge, the centre of scholarship, and because he had no money to go as a student, he went as a teacher. His subject was Newton's Optics, of all improbable things, and he lectured so brilliantly that his lectures were always packed. Young John Harrison, the clock-maker, copied out all his lecture notes. However, Saunderson was not always successful;

The plaque in Thurlstone: 'Here was born Dr Nicholas Saunderson, 1682'.

Horace Walpole, son of the first prime minister, wrote that he had been unable to learn his tables, and Saunderson had said to him, 'Young man, it would be cheating you to take your money; for you can never learn what I am trying to teach you.'

Saunderson became well respected, wrote a treatise on algebra, and in 1711 he was given an MA by special mandate from Queen Anne. He was elected Lucasian Professor of Mathematics, the position that Newton had held until 1703, and one of the most prestigious maths jobs in the world. But perhaps the most remarkable thing about this remarkable man was that according to legend he

Nicholas Saunderson, the blind mathematician, learned to read by feeling the letters on the gravestones in Penistone churchyard.

learned to read by feeling the letters on the gravestones in Penistone churchyard.

There's a plaque near the phone box in Thurlstone, and the churchyard at Penistone has gravestones that he must have read by touch.

42. GEORGE PARKER BIDDER, THE CALCULATING BOY

There have been a number of stories about mathematical prodigies – children and adults who could do any calculation in their heads in an instant, for whom lightning mental arithmetic seemed to be a pleasure. Among the most amazing was George Parker Bidder.

George was born on 14 June 1806 in Moretonhampstead on the edge of Dartmoor, the third son of a stonemason. He was supposed to go to the village school, but in fact played truant most of the time. His elder brother taught him to count up to ten, and then up to a hundred; that was the limit of his mathematical education. An old blacksmith used to work across the road; from about the age of six George used to sit in his workshop and help operate the bellows. People who came in found he could quickly sing out the answers to simple sums. They would say, 'Thirty-seven times sixty-nine', and without a pause he'd pipe up, 'Two thousand five hundred and fifty-three.' He could easily do two-figure multiplication sums, and just about managed three figures. Soon he was able to answer tricky problems: *If one man takes twenty days to do a job, and another takes thirty days, how long would they take working together?* The answer came instantly: 'Twelve days.'

His dad began to take him round to local fairs, exhibiting him as 'The Calculating Boy' and charging money for admission. George soon became famous, and travelled to Brighton, Cheltenham, Tewkesbury, Dudley, Worcester, Birmingham, Oxford, Cambridge, Norwich and London; the Duke of Kent asked him to multiply 7,953 by 4,648; he quickly

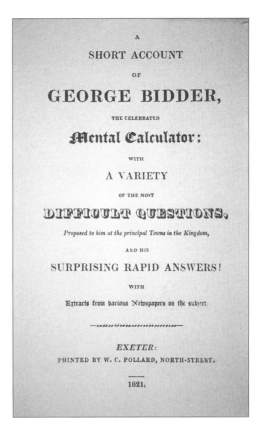

A
SHORT ACCOUNT
OF
GEORGE BIDDER,
THE CELEBRATED
Mental Calculator:
WITH
A VARIETY
OF THE MOST
DIFFICULT QUESTIONS,
Proposed to him at the principal Towns in the Kingdom,
AND HIS
SURPRISING RAPID ANSWERS!
WITH
Extracts from various Newspapers on the subject.

EXETER:
PRINTED BY W. C. POLLARD, NORTH-STREET.

1821.

Bidder became quite a celebrity.

answered 36,965,544. When he was about ten he was summoned to appear before Queen Charlotte, who asked him, *How many days would a snail be creeping, at the rate of 8 feet per day, from the Land's End in Cornwall to Farret's Head in Scotland, the distance by admeasurement being 838 miles?* He answered 553,080. The famous astronomer Sir William Herschel asked him, *Light travels from the Sun to the Earth in 8 minutes, and the Sun being 98 million miles off, if Light would take 6 years and 4 months travelling from the nearest fixed star, how far is that star from the Earth, reckoning 365 days and 6 hours to each year, and 28 days to each month?* Answer: 40,633,740 million miles.

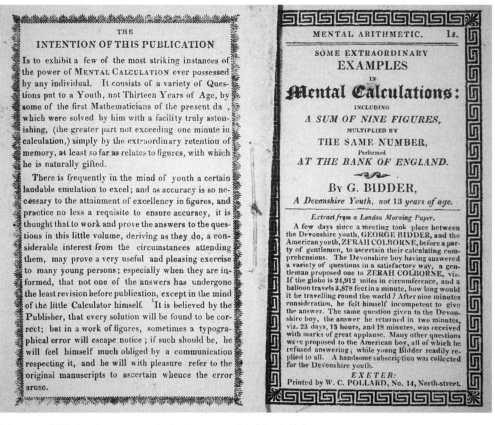

THE
INTENTION OF THIS PUBLICATION

Is to exhibit a few of the most striking instances of the power of MENTAL CALCULATION ever possessed by any individual. It consists of a variety of Questions put to a Youth, not Thirteen Years of Age, by some of the first Mathematicians of the present da , which were solved by him with a facility truly astonishing, (the greater part not exceeding one minute in calculation,) simply by the extraordinary retention of memory, at least so far as relates to figures, with which he is naturally gifted.

There is frequently in the mind of youth a certain laudable emulation to excel; and as accuracy is so necessary to the attainment of excellency in figures, and practice no less a requisite to ensure accuracy, it is thought that to work and prove the answers to the questions in this little volume, deriving as they do, a considerable interest from the circumstances attending them, may prove a very useful and pleasing exercise to many young persons; especially when they are informed, that not one of the answers has undergone the least revision before publication, except in the mind of the little Calculator himself. It is believed by the Publisher, that every solution will be found to be correct; but in a work of figures, sometimes a typographical error will escape notice ; if such should be, he will feel himself much obliged by a communication respecting it, and he will with pleasure refer to the original manuscripts to ascertain whence the error arose.

MENTAL ARITHMETIC.   1s.

SOME EXTRAORDINARY
EXAMPLES
IN
Mental Calculations:
INCLUDING
A SUM OF NINE FIGURES,
MULTIPLIED BY
THE SAME NUMBER,
Performed
AT THE BANK OF ENGLAND.

By G. BIDDER,
A Devonshire Youth, not 13 years of age.

Extract from a London Morning Paper.
A few days since a meeting took place between the Devonshire youth, GEORGE BIDDER, and the American youth, ZERAH COLBORNE, before a party of gentlemen, to ascertain their calculating comprehensions. The Devonshire boy having answered a variety of questions in a satisfactory way, a gentleman proposed one to ZERAH COLBORNE, viz. If the globe is 24,912 miles in circumference, and a balloon travels 3,878 feet in a minute, how long would it be travelling round the world ? After nine minutes consideration, he felt himself incompetent to give the answer. The same question given to the Devonshire boy, the answer he returned in two minutes, viz. 23 days, 13 hours, and 18 minutes, was received with marks of great applause. Many other questions were proposed to the American boy, all of which he refused answering ; while young Bidder readily replied to all. A handsome subscription was collected for the Devonshire youth.
EXETER:
Printed by W. C. POLLARD, No. 14, North-street.

This account of Bidder's genius was supposed to inspire young people to follow in his footsteps.

George produced these answers with amazing speed – taking perhaps a minute for the longer sums – and with stunning accuracy. Rarely did he make a mistake. Books were published of the questions he was asked, although since they must have been produced after the events, they carry no proof of his speed or accuracy. On a show visit to the Bank of England, when he was twelve, he was asked to multiply together two nine-digit numbers: $257,689,435 \times 356,875,649$. He got the answer right, but it took him thirteen minutes.

He tried to explain his processes of mental arithmetic, in two lectures to the Institution of Civil Engineers in 1856. He said he did not have a remarkable memory; nor was he a great mathematician, as he found to his cost when he was struggling with a maths degree at Cambridge. Mental arithmetic was a skill, he said, that anyone of reasonable capacity could learn. The main rule, he said, is to take the steps of a calculation in such a way as to minimize the use of the registering power of the mind, because remembering intermediates is what limits calculating ability. He always began at the left, and added after each multiplication. So, if asked for 89×73 he would say instantly 6,497, but to spell it out in stages, his process would be 80×70 and remember, 80×3, then add this and remember the total, 9×70 then add and remember, 9×3 and add to give the answer. He was frequently asked to work out square roots or cube roots, but was greatly helped by the knowledge that the answer would be a whole number, because the asker would have squared or cubed a whole number, in order to know what the answer would be. The first square root he was asked for was of 390,625. He later said: 'It occurred to me immediately that 5 must be the last figure, and that since 600 times 600 is 360,000, the first figure must be 6.' So he needed only the middle digit, and quickly found that 1 worked; so the answer was 615. So, asked to find the cube root of 188,132,517, he knew that 500 cubed would be 125 million and 600 cubed would be 216 million; so the answer must be in between. He also happened to know that 73 was the only number between 1 and 100 whose cube ended in 17. So he guessed 573 – checked – and it was the answer.

His calculating started when he was a little boy, lying in bed at night, thinking about numbers. He loved to count to ten and then on from there. He would play with adding – six and six is the same as six and four and two, the same as ten and two, the same as twelve. He was glad he had never been taught any rules for doing sums; because he had worked them out for himself he understood them thoroughly.

In the first draft version of his lecture, all the numbers are written out in full – sixty-seven times ninety-three. When he was young, he was always given his challenges out loud, and he was being exhibited before he learned to read; later he found the process much slower if he had to read digits on paper. So seeing Arabic numerals actually hindered his calculations.

Being exhibited as a boy did not ruin his life. He surveyed for the Ordnance Survey,

became an engineer and made use of his genius. He was a friend and from 1834 often a partner of Robert Stephenson; they built many railways together. He was one of the founders in 1846 of the Electric Telegraph Company. He was also involved in the building of the sewers of London around 1860. He built railways in Norway and in Denmark, where he also introduced gas lighting. Unlike his contemporary Isambard Kingdom Brunel, he completed his projects on time and within budget. Indeed the wonderful Clifton Suspension Bridge was unfinished when Brunel died because they had run out of money, and it was George Parker Bidder who raised the money and got the job finished in the early 1860s. He also invented the railway swing bridge. While building the Norwich & Brandon railway line in 1845 he had to cross the River Wensum, which was used by many boats coming into the port of Norwich. So he constructed the Trowse Swing Bridge, which lasted until 1905.

He retained his calculating ability throughout his life. In September 1878 the Revd E.M. Johnstone came to visit; they talked about light giving notions of the infinitely great and the infinitely small; that it travels at almost 190,000 miles per second through space, and that red light has 36,918 wavelengths in one inch. Johnstone wondered how many waves from a red object would strike the eye in one second, and reached for pencil and paper, but George stopped him, and said, 'You need not work it out; the number of vibrations will be 444 billion, 433,651 million, and 200,000.' And this was the day before he died.

George Parker Bidder's birthplace in Moretonhampstead was about 20 yards west of where the information office now is, on the site of the present bakery.

43. CHARLES HUTTON AND THE INVENTION OF CONTOUR LINES

In 1774 Nevil Maskelyne went to Schiehallion in the highlands of Scotland and spent four uncomfortable months measuring the positions of observatories north and south of the mountain. Using Newton's idea of the Attraction of Mountains, he wanted to calculate the mass of the Earth (*see* page 82). Because this required some tricky calculations he went for help to a mathematician, Charles Hutton.

Born in Newcastle in 1737, Charles Hutton became a coal-miner, but was so bright that they made him a teacher, and then Professor of Mathematics at the Royal Military Academy in Woolwich. He wrote a paper in 1778 'On the force of exploded gunpowder and the velocities of balls'.

CHARLES HUTTON, LL.D., F.R.S.

London. Published by Hodgson & Co. 112 Newgate Street.

—1824—

Charles Hutton.

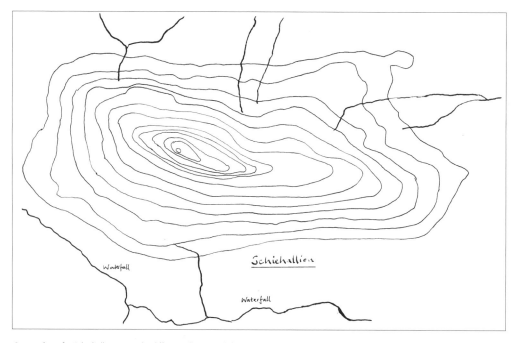

Contour lines for Schiehallion. Note the difference from Maskelyne's map on page 84.

784   *Mr.* HUTTON's *Calculations to aſcertain*

our experiment: or $\frac{4}{13}$, or between $\frac{1}{3}$ and $\frac{1}{4}$ of the whole magnitude will be metal; and conſequently $\frac{10}{17}$, or nearly $\frac{3}{5}$ of the diameter of the earth, is the central or metalline part.

Knowing then the mean denſity of the earth in compariſon with water, and the denſities of all the planets relatively to the earth, we can now aſſign the proportions of the denſities of all of them as compared to water, after the manner of a common table of ſpecific gravities. And the numbers expreſſing their relative denſities, in reſpect of water, will be as below, ſuppoſing the denſities of the planets, as compared to each other, to be as laid down in Mr. DE LA LANDE's aſtronomy.

Water . . . 1
The Sun . . $1\frac{4}{15}$
Mercury . . $9\frac{1}{6}$
Venus . . . $5\frac{11}{15}$
The earth . . $4\frac{1}{2}$
Mars . . . . $3\frac{3}{7}$
The Moon . . $3\frac{1}{11}$
Jupiter . . . $1\frac{1}{14}$
Saturn . . . $\frac{12}{31}$

Thus then we have brought to a concluſion the computation of this important experiment, and, it is hoped, with no inconſiderable degree of accuracy. But it is the

firſt

the mean Denſity of the Earth.   785

firſt experiment of the kind which has been ſo minutely and circumſtantially treated; and firſt attempts are ſeldom ſo perfect and juſt as ſucceeding endeavours afterwards render them. And, beſides, a frequent repetition of the ſame experiment, and a coincidence of reſults, afford that firm dependance on the concluſions and ſatiſfaction to the mind, which can ſcarcely ever be had from a ſingle trial, however carefully it may be executed. For thoſe reaſons it is to be wiſhed, that the world may not reſt ſatisfied barely with what has been done in this inſtance, but that they will repeat the experiment in other ſituations, and in other countries, with all the care and preciſion that it may be poſſible to give to it, till an uniformity of concluſions ſhall be formed, ſufficient to eſtabliſh the point in queſtion beyond any reaſonable poſſibility of doubt.' What has been already done in the preſent caſe will render any future repetition more eaſy and perfect. But improvements may be made, perhaps both in the mode of computation and in the ſurvey; in the latter, eſpecially, there certainly may. Some improvements of this kind I have hinted at in ſome parts of this paper, which with others I ſhall here collect together, that they may readily be ſeen in one point of view. They are principally theſe. Procure one baſe, or more if convenient, very accurately meaſured, in ſuch ſituation, that

VOL. LXVIII.   5 E   as

Hutton calculated the densities of all the known objects in the solar system.

Maskelyne's surveyors had measured the altitude of dozens of points on the ground on and around Schiehallion, and Maskelyne wanted to know the size and shape of the mountain. Hutton reckoned that his first task was to represent the mountain on a flat map. He had the brilliant idea of joining together all the points of equal height; he wrote in his paper that he did this with a very faint pencil. The result was remarkable; he could see at once the shape of the mountain. Where the contours are close together the mountain is steep, and there is clearly a long ridge running along the top. Hutton's lines are what we now call contour lines.

To measure the volume of the mountain he imagined the whole thing was made of hundreds of thin vertical columns of rock; then he used his contour lines to estimate the height of each column, which allowed him to calculate the volume of the mountain. To work out its mass he assumed the whole thing had a density of 2.5 g/cm³, the same as the surface rocks.

Hutton's calculations gave a value for the density of the Earth of 4.5 g/cm³, and for the mass of the Earth as about 5,000,000,000,000,000,000,000 tonnes, which was within about 20 per cent of today's accepted value. This was the first measurement of the mass of the Earth; twenty years were to go before anyone did it better; and meanwhile Charles Hutton had invented contour lines, which have been used on maps ever since.

Schiehallion is south-west of Tummel Bridge – GR 272754; a plaque by the picnic area on the small road north-east of the mountain describes the great event.

44. GEORGE GREEN, THE MATHEMATICAL MILLER

In 1928 Albert Einstein sent a telegram to the University of Nottingham to commemorate the centenary of the publication of a remarkable essay in mathematical physics. Two years later, in June 1930, he visited Nottingham in person to give a public lecture in the evening, but during the afternoon he planned to go and pay homage at the grave of George Green, the author of the essay. Unfortunately he missed his train, and never saw the grave. However, he delivered his lecture to all the assembled ladies and gentlemen of Nottingham, on one of the hottest evenings of the year. Wearing full evening dress, Einstein spoke for two hours in German on General Relativity, which must have been unintelligible to almost the entire audience. So who was George Green, and why did his essay so impress Einstein?

George was born in Nottingham on 13 July 1793. At the age of eight he went to school, but eighteen months later he left, in order to join his dad in the bakery. In 1807 George's father decided to cut out the middle man, and make his own flour; so he built himself a windmill at Sneinton. It was one of the first brick mills in the area. Beautifully restored, Green's Mill is still making flour today.

A miller was employed to run the mill, and the miller's house was built on the side of the mill itself – the traces of plaster from the front room are still visible on the exterior brickwork. George was fourteen when the mill was built, and he probably played with the miller's

daughter Jane, who was a few years younger. He never went any further to do his courting; George and Jane produced seven children, and are buried side by side in the churchyard below the mill. However, for some reason they were never married; perhaps his father threatened to disinherit him if he married the miller's daughter!

So George Green was comfortably established, with a partner and children and a prosperous business, but he wanted more; he wanted to leave his mark on the world. And so, astonishingly, he decided to become a mathematician! No one knows why he took this decision, nor how he got hold of the books, but apparently he went up to the top of the mill and studied mathematical textbooks 'in the hours stolen from my sleep', as he put it.

Most of the great advances in mathematics have been achieved by people in their late teens or early twenties; the barely adult brain appears to be the best cradle for brilliant steps forward in the most abstract of sciences. Newton, for example, made all his great discoveries in 1665–6, when he was aged twenty-three or twenty-four. There's a famous story of the 21-year-old French genius Evariste Galois, who discovered group theory; in 1832 he was challenged to a duel. He sat up the night before writing down his ideas on group theory so that they would not be lost, and died in the duel in the morning. Yet George Green left school at the age of nine and did not even start thinking about mathematics until he was in his thirties, so the fact that he discovered some

Green's Mill in Sneinton where he worked at mathematics 'in the hours stolen from my sleep'.

astonishing new ideas is all the more remarkable.

As far as we know he had no colleagues or friends with whom he could discuss his notions, but in 1828 he wrote a long original paper with the snappy title *An essay on the application of mathematical analysis to the theories of electricity and magnetism.* He had this privately printed in Nottingham, and sold copies at *7s 6d.* There were just fifty-one subscribers, mostly family and friends.

This slim volume almost sank without trace. No one heard about it in far-off Cambridge or London. But luck was on George's side, for twenty years later a seventeen-year-old Irishman called William Thomson came across a reference to 'the ingenious essay by Mr Green of Nottingham', and managed to get hold of a copy the night before setting off for Paris. He read it on the stagecoach, with growing excitement, and told all his French physicist friends about its conclusions. They were stunned, for they discovered that this dusty essay had already solved several of the problems that were holding them up. In fact the essay could hardly have

fallen into better hands; Thomson was himself a genius who made many advances in several branches of physics. He became Lord Kelvin, and was Professor of Natural Philosophy at the University of Glasgow for fifty-three years.

The gold in this essay lay in two nuggets, which came to be called Green's Functions and Green's Theorem. Green's Functions are a complicated mathematical trick that helps to make physics problems possible to solve, essentially by knocking off a dimension. Measuring the surface area of Australia on a three-dimensional globe would be difficult, but if you could knock off a dimension and measure it on a flat map it would be much easier. Green's Functions have been useful in the fields of gravity, superconductors, semiconductors, magnetism and many other branches of high-powered physics. That's why Einstein was so impressed. And these amazing ideas were conjured up by a middle-aged mill-owner, in the hours stolen from his sleep!

There's a science centre and coffee shop at George Green's windmill, which still makes flour at Sneinton, east Nottingham; open Wed–Sun, 10–5; 01602 503635.

45. GEORGE BOOLE, AND HIS VISION IN A FIELD IN DONCASTER

Boole's vision in a field in Doncaster.

Life today is full of computers; sometimes they seem to run our lives. But they might not run at all if it had not been for a vision experienced by a seventeen-year-old assistant teacher in a field in Doncaster.

George Boole was born in Lincoln on 4 November 1815. His father was a shoemaker, but probably spent too little time making shoes and too much messing about with scientific instruments and mathematical ideas. However, he did succeed in giving his son a lust for learning. Young George was a precocious schoolboy, and astonished the readers of his local newspaper by producing an elegant translation of some Greek verse –

so elegant that another pedantic reader wrote to the editor and protested that such a young lad could not possibly have produced such a translation without a good deal of help. He probably hoped to go to university, but in 1831 his father's business failed, and so fifteen-year-old George had to go out to work in order to support the family.

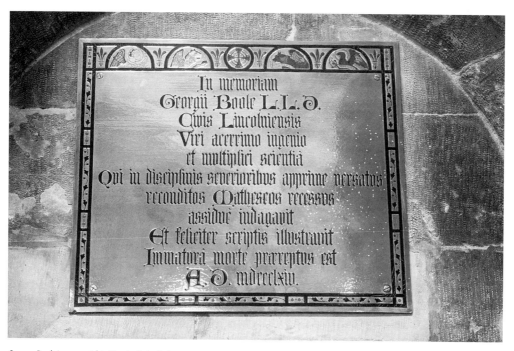

George Boole's memorial in Lincoln Cathedral.

George Boole memorial window, Lincoln Cathedral.

Unable to find a job in Lincoln, he walked 40 miles north to Doncaster, and in July secured the post of usher, or assistant teacher, in Mr Heigham's School in South Parade. He did not enjoy being so far from home; it must have been at least two days' walk. He was lonely, and wrote home often, complaining that no one in Doncaster made gooseberry pies as good as his mother's. He was also rather unhappy at the school, a strict Wesleyan establishment where religion came first, and nothing else must be allowed to interfere. Some of the parents suspected George of reading mathematics books on Sundays, and even worse, he was accused of doing sums in chapel!

One problem was that he loved to read, but had no easy access to a library or other source of free books; so he had to buy his own. Because he didn't have much money, he always bought books that took a long time to read and therefore provided good value. He found the best of all were textbooks of mathematics, which took many hours to plod through. Later in life, he claimed that this was how he became seriously interested in mathematics. When he was neither teaching nor absorbing mathematics, he liked to go walking. He was lucky, for directly across the Great North Road he found Town Fields, a great expanse of common land, ideal for walking off the pain of a teenage exile. This was where he had his vision – a revelation that changed the world.

One cold day in January 1833 George was walking along thinking, when he was suddenly struck by an astonishing idea. He often talked about the moment later in life, and compared the experience with that of Saul on the road to Damascus. It changed his life, and it changed our lives too. George had learned from his reading that mathematics was highly successful in describing the working of the physical world; ever since Newton, scientists had been applying mathematics to all sorts of moving systems – from cannon balls to planets – and had found their motions could be described and predicted using simple mathematical laws. George's idea was this: if mathematics could describe the physical world, could it also describe the mental world? If mathematical principles explained the functioning of cogwheels of machines, could they also explain the cogwheels of thought? Could he develop the maths to unravel the human mind?

At first this was only a flash of inspiration, and it took him fourteen years to work out the details, but eventually he wrote a long essay called *The mathematical analysis of logic, being an essay towards a calculus of deductive reasoning* (1847), and then a book called *An investigation into the laws of thought* (1854). These created tremendous interest. Bertrand Russell said: 'Pure mathematics was discovered by Boole, in a work which he called The Laws of Thought.' In his day he was regarded as the greatest logician since Aristotle.

According to Boole's system, logical problems could be expressed as algebraic equations, and therefore solved by mechanical manipulation of symbols according to formal rules. There were only two values – 0 and 1, or False and True – and logical ideas could be added to one another: if (day = Wednesday) and (time = afternoon) then the shops are

shut. The shops remain open if either value is False.

Although Boole thought he had solved the mystery of the human mind, others were not convinced. Nevertheless, Boolean algebra was such an elegant system that it became widely known, admired and used. And in the 1930s, when Claude Shannon was trying to build the world's first computer at Massachusetts Institute of Technology, he found that it precisely described the behaviour of an array of electrical switches – each of which has just two positions, Off or On.

Shannon was working on the mathematics of information, and had reduced every choice to Yes or No. He represented these with a binary code, and called each unit of information a 'binary digit' or bit. So the fundamental ideas for electronic computers came straight from Boolean algebra.

George Boole was fired by Mr Heigham within a few weeks of his revelation, but he went back to Lincoln and started a school of his own. He married Mary Everest, niece of the surveyor of northern India, who gave his name to the world's highest mountain, and they produced a horde of successful children. He went on to become Professor of Mathematics at the University of Cork. Maybe he did not solve the mystery of the human mind, but the logic of every computer today is based on the idea that came to him in that flash of inspiration, in a field in Doncaster.

You can still go for an inspiring walk in Town Fields, Doncaster. Boole is commemorated by a window and brass plaque in Lincoln Cathedral and a plaque on the wall of 3 Pottergate, nearby.

	S	M	T	W	T	F	S	S	M	T	W	T	F	S	S	M	T	W	T	F	S	S	M	T	W	T	F	S
Jan	1	2	3	4	5	6	7	8	9	10	11	12	13	14	15	16	17	18	19	20	21	22	23	24	25	26	27	28
Feb	1	2	3	4	5	6	7	8	9	10	11	12	13	14	15	16	17	18	19	20	21	22	23	24	25	26	27	28
Mar	1	2	3	4	5	6	7	8	9	10	11	12	13	14	15	16	17	18	19	20	21	22	23	24	25	26	27	28
Apr	1	2	3	4	5	6	7	8	9	10	11	12	13	14	15	16	17	18	19	20	21	22	23	24	25	26	27	28
May	1	2	3	4	5	6	7	8	9	10	11	12	13	14	15	16	17	18	19	20	21	22	23	24	25	26	27	28
Jun	1	2	3	4	5	6	7	8	9	10	11	12	13	14	15	16	17	18	19	20	21	22	23	24	25	26	27	28
Sol	1	2	3	4	5	6	7	8	9	10	11	12	13	14	15	16	17	18	19	20	21	22	23	24	25	26	27	28
Jul	1	2	3	4	5	6	7	8	9	10	11	12	13	14	15	16	17	18	19	20	21	22	23	24	25	26	27	28
Aug	1	2	3	4	5	6	7	8	9	10	11	12	13	14	15	16	17	18	19	20	21	22	23	24	25	26	27	28
Sep	1	2	3	4	5	6	7	8	9	10	11	12	13	14	15	16	17	18	19	20	21	22	23	24	25	26	27	28
Oct	1	2	3	4	5	6	7	8	9	10	11	12	13	14	15	16	17	18	19	20	21	22	23	24	25	26	27	28
Nov	1	2	3	4	5	6	7	8	9	10	11	12	13	14	15	16	17	18	19	20	21	22	23	24	25	26	27	28
Dec	1	2	3	4	5	6	7	8	9	10	11	12	13	14	15	16	17	18	19	20	21	22 (bd)	23	24	25	26	27	28

Moses Bruine Cotsworth's Rational Calendar.

46. MOSES BRUINE COTSWORTH AND HIS RATIONAL CALENDAR

Our calendar is a mess. We have seven months with thirty-one days, four months with thirty days, and one with twenty-eight or twenty-nine. Only February ever has an exact number of weeks. All this

would have been sorted out if only the world had accepted the ideas of Moses Bruine Cotsworth.

Cotsworth, born at Acomb near York in 1859, worked as a goods clerk for the North Eastern Railway in York, but he was obsessed with numbers. He became a statistician, and used to get up at 4 a.m. to work on his calculations before going in to the NER. This led to various books of calculations and ready-reckoners, but his *magnum opus* was the *Rational Almanac* published in 1904. All the information you needed was in the table inside the front cover of his book, but he actually wrote 471 more pages, to justify the idea.

Cotsworth said the first day of every

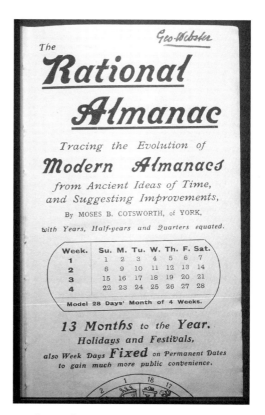

The *Rational Almanac*: pocket-sized if you had very long pockets.

One of Cotsworth's aims was to have thirteen months, each with twenty-eight days.

The Rational Almanac.

Without disturbing the accepted Gregorian lengths of Years now used, the advantages of the Proposed Permanent Almanac could be easily realised by 3 simple steps:—

1—From Christmas Day, 1916, cease naming Christmas Day by any week-day name, and merely call it " Christmas Day," which could be thus set apart as the extra yearly day, fitted into the last week of the year as a duplicate Sunday to permanently combine the week-end holiday with Christmas, and get rid of the troublesome and unbusinesslike changing of week-day names for dates throughout future years.

By naming " Leap Day " as a Public Holiday without any week-day name, justice would be done to salaried servants, whilst maintaining fixed day names for each date.

2—Let Easter, Whitsuntide and the other movable Festivals be FIXED (as Christmas is) to always fall on the fixed Dates to be arranged for 1916, or such other Permanent Dates as will best suit the convenience, welfare and pleasure of the People.—Easter, our longest " open-air " public holiday, would be better for the Church and people if celebrated in more ideal weather towards May.

3—Divide the 52 weeks of the Year *into* 13 *months of* 4 *weeks each* for greater utility and business facility, by inserting a Mid-Summer month (Sol) as shown below.

How Christmas would be arranged.

month should be a Sunday, and every month should have exactly four weeks. There should be thirteen months in the year. He proposed to use the existing months, and add an extra one called 'Sol', the month of the sun, between June and July. Thirteen months of four weeks each makes fifty-two weeks, or 364 days. Christmas Day would always be on Sunday 22 December, and he proposed that the following day, Boxing Day, should simply be another Sunday. Then New Year's Eve would be Saturday, and everything would fit. Leap years would be catered for the same way – with two consecutive Sundays. The result is a wonderfully simple year planner. Any particular date will always be

the same day every month – and every year. The 13th would always be a Friday, and birthdays would always fall on the same day of the week.

Cotsworth was passionate about his rational calendar. He spent years promoting it, travelled to more than sixty countries, and was appointed to the League of Nations Committee on Calendar Reform, and became Director of the International Fixed Calendar League. Despite all this, he failed to change the world, but he did convince George Eastman, head of Kodak, and until a few years ago all Kodak employees were paid in thirteen monthly instalments.

DOMESTIC BLISS

One popular image of inventions focuses on those household gadgets that are supposed to make our lives easier. Not only are they said to take all the work out of cleaning or polishing, but they allegedly give us masses of extra leisure time. What happened to all that leisure time? Are there really people sitting at home languidly watching television while their gadgets do all the work? Or do the gadgets merely create extra work for us to do?

This section of the book focuses on household ideas that fall into two broad categories: 'Wish I'd thought of that!' and 'I don't believe it!' Some are sensible, some are absurd, and some made people rich, although not always the inventors.

47. BED AND BREAKFAST

Dr William Oliver was an eminent physician who settled in Bath in 1725 and developed a rich and successful practice. He helped to build – and for many years ran – the Royal Mineral Water Hospital. During the course of his work he invented a biscuit with a special recipe as part of a diet he regularly prescribed. Before he died, on 17 March 1764, he gave the secret recipe for his biscuit to his coachman Atkins, along with £100 and ten sacks of the finest wheat flour. Atkins opened a shop on Green Street, marketed the biscuit as the Bath Oliver, and made a fortune. Buy a packet today, and you can see the portrait of Dr Oliver stamped on every biscuit.

One of the most ambitious of the domestic inventors was Sarah Guppy of Bristol. Thomas Guppy was an iron founder, who was a colleague of Isambard Kingdom Brunel, and in particular cast for him the pipes for the South Devon atmospheric railway (*see* page 31). Tom's brother Samuel Guppy was a successful merchant with smart premises in Queen Square. He took out several patents for the manufacture of soap and nails, and it seems that his wife Sarah decided that this patenting business was good fun – and could be lucrative – so she had a go too, and altogether took out three patents.

Her first, in 1811, was ambitious; she patented the Suspension Bridge. Now suspension bridges had been built for some hundreds if not thousands of years – for example by the Incas in Peru – although the major suspension bridges in Britain, including the Menai Bridge,

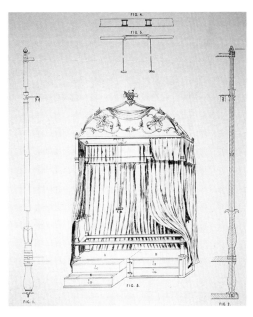

Sarah Guppy's patent bed, with exercise handles and steps to prevent dust gathering underneath.

the Conwy Bridge, and the Clifton Suspension Bridge all came later. Presumably Telford and Brunel claimed earlier precedents and avoided paying Mrs Guppy for the right to use her ideas.

In 1831 – after her husband had died – Sarah Guppy patented an ingenious bedstead with special steps which slid out from below the sides of the bed; these both made climbing in and out easier, and prevented dust from gathering under the bed. But the bedstead also had 'a set of springs and rollers to be used for exercise when in bed'. Her idea seems to have been to do pull-ups without having to get up in the morning!

Her simplest and most alluring patent, however, was that of 1812, for 'Certain improvements in tea and coffee urns'. She is fairly precise about the construction; she makes her tea urn in any

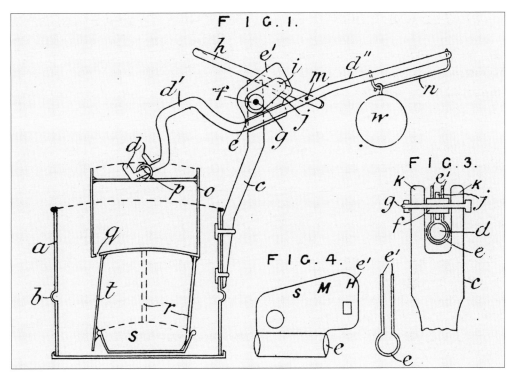

Dr Gaddes's automatic egg-boiler. The egg sits in the container 'S', shown in the cooking position. He simplified the design a couple of years later.

of the 'usual forms and constructions', but she cunningly modifies it with a simultaneous egg-boiler – a basket suspended from the lid so that the eggs sit in the water.

Her genius didn't end there, though, because in the lid of the urn she made 'an elegant and convenient support for a plate or dish or other vessel to contain toast or other article of food or refreshment'. In other words, Sarah Guppy's modified tea urn allows you to make tea and boiled eggs in one operation, and keeps your toast warm at the same time. How can we survive without one?

However, different people have different problems at breakfast, and Dr

Thomas Gaddes, dentist of Station Parade, Harrogate, was clearly worried about being called away – perhaps by demanding patients – before he could take his eggs out of the boiling water, so they became as hard as rocks. So in the late 1890s he devised an automatic egg-boiler, which actually took the egg out of the boiling water at the moment when it was perfectly cooked.

The diagrams he provided in his patents show the simplicity of the idea. The regulator h is adjusted on the lever arm into notch H, M, or S, according to whether you like your egg hard, medium, or soft, and the sliding weight is moved to the top slot if two eggs are to be boiled. Water trickles out of the reservoir, so that the basket holding the egg slowly rises. When enough water has run out, the slots in regulator h tip just below the horizontal, the weight slides down, and the egg is pulled rapidly out of the water. Indeed the egg is then slightly cooled by the water which continues to drain, so that it rapidly stops cooking.

Had Thomas Gaddes and Sarah Guppy lived closer together in time and place, they might have found they had much in common!

In about 1840 Mrs Annabel Coote of Bristol invented a mobile sheep-wash, which seems to have been a sort of wicker basket for holding the animal still while it was scrubbed. History does not relate how successful it was.

In 1932 Gilbert Malloch of Perth invented a combined walking-stick, salmon gaff, landing net and camera tripod – a sort of fishing equivalent of the Swiss Army knife. Mr Malloch was in the business of selling fishing gear, so perhaps he had spotted a genuine marketing opportunity.

Gilbert Malloch with his multi-purpose invention.

William Oliver's portrait hangs in the main staircase of the Royal Mineral Water Hospital in Bath, which he helped to build. Thomas Gaddes's premises at 104 Station Parade, Harrogate, are still there.

48. CHRISTOPHER PINCHBECK AND HIS NOCTURNAL REMEMBRANCER

When you wake up in the middle of the night you often experience a curious semi-conscious mental state, called the hypnopompic state by some psycho-logists. Often you have vivid images, and occasionally what seem to be brilliant thoughts. But by the morning they are all forgotten. The best way of trying to recall those flashes of genius seems to be to write them down; so you need to keep a pencil and paper by the bed. However, one potential problem remains; if you try to write down your pearl of wisdom in the dark, you might write on top of the previous idea, and thus render both illegible. This was the difficulty solved by the 'nocturnal remembrancer' of Christopher Pinchbeck.

Christopher Pinchbeck was born about 1710. His father – also called Christopher – made clocks and clever musical toys, and invented a new metal alloy, a mixture of copper and zinc that looked like gold and could be used in cheap jewellery; it is still called pinchbeck. Christopher Jnr was something of a mechanical genius. He won a gold medal for inventing a self-acting pneumatic brake for cranes; he made a very complicated astronomical clock with four dials, which found its way to Buckingham Palace; and he devised a candlestick which ensured that the candle always stayed upright, and therefore avoided spilling molten wax on the floor.

He patented his nocturnal remembrancer in 1768, and covered all

A.D. 1768.—N° 899.   **3**

Pinchbeck's Memoranda Tablets.

skin, ivory, slate, and of every other material made use of for the leaves of
tablets or pocket books, and whose case or outside is made of gold, silver,
ivory, tortoishell, leather, and likewise of every material of which the outside or cases of other tablets or pocket books are made; and within about half
5 an inch of the top of this case, where the tablets or leaves are put in, a hole is
cut on both sides, about one quarter of an inch wide, quite across the case,
to within a little more than the eighth of an inch on each side, which holes
are a guide for you to write whatever occurs on the leaf on each side that is
outermost or nearest to you, without your pencil slipping, and to prevent your
10 making confusion by writing again in the same place.   All the leaves (which
are fastned together by a small loose ring which passes through the center
of them, within less than a quarter of an inch of the top) have notches cut
on one of their sides, at about a quarter of an inch asunder, and a spring
with a returned nose to it, which goes into those notches to hold them firm,
15 and is fastned on one side the case, and which, by pushing a small button
which is fixt to it, and comes through on that side of the case, is relieved at
pleasure, so as to be pulled up to another notch by the ring.   And if more
thoughts should occur than two sides will hold, by pressing the button of the
said spring, pulling the tablets quite out, and turning over the leaves which
20 are all held together by the above-mentioned ring, you have double the
number of sides to write on than your case will hold leaves, the notches in
all answering to the nose of the spring ; and on the other side of the case the
pencil is put in a hole for that purpose.

In witness whereof, I, the said Christopher Pinchbeck have hereunto set
25   my hand and seal, this Eighth day of July, in the year of our Lord
One thousand seven hundred and sixty-eight, and in the eighth year of
the reign of our said Sovereign Lord George the Third, by the grace
of God of Great Britain, France, and Ireland King, Defender of the
Faith.

30   CHRIST^R PINCHBECK.   (L.S.)

Sealed and delivered (being first duly
stampt) in the presence of us,
the words (and on the other side
of the case the pencil is put in a
35 hole for that purpose) being first
interlined.

SAM^L BLACKSHAW.
BIGOE HENZELL,
Clerk to Henry Rooke, Esquire.

Pinchbeck's 1768 patent for the 'Nocturnal Remembrancer'.

manner of possible developments by describing it in fancy terms. Thus of the notepad he says, 'a set of tablets, whose leaves are of asses' skin, ivory, slate, and of every other material made use of for the leaves of tablets or pocket books, and whose case or outside is made of gold, silver, ivory, tortoiseshell, leather, and likewise of every material of which the outside or cases of other tablets or pocket books are made . . .'.

Basically, however, it was a notepad sliding up and down inside a case, and held in place by a spring-loaded catch resting in a notch. The case had a slot in the front, which you could feel in the dark, and through which you could write your brilliant idea; the front of the case masked the rest of the pad. When you had written down an idea, you slid the pad up the case to the next notch, so that your previous idea was covered by the case, and a fresh patch of pad exposed in the slot. Thus even in complete darkness you could write down your ideas and be sure of never going over something you had written before.

What is most amusing about this device is that even though it's really just a notepad he called it a 'nocturnal remembrancer', as though the gadget was going to do the remembering. I am reminded of those gadgets you buy by mail-order today that promise to do everything, and turn out to be just a piece of string and a pencil.

49. STRIKE A LIGHT! JOHN WALKER

It is a cliché to say that we take many modern inventions for granted, but in the case of the friction match it is particularly justifiable. Life without electricity would be pretty hard, but you can manage with fire: candles for light, and gas, coal or wood for heating and cooking. But things would get very uncomfortable if you couldn't actually light your fire. Yet before John Walker's invention of 1826, there wasn't a reliable, instantaneous method of lighting a fire.

Fire-making technology had been around for thousands of years. The earliest methods relied on friction, typically between two bits of wood. Although it is possible to do this by simply spinning one piece of wood against another using your hands, if you try you will find it difficult to get enough speed. So the first real fire making machine was the Fire Drill. It looked like the bow part of a bow-and-arrow, and you used it by wrapping its string round a pencil-shaped piece of hard

Strike a light!

wood, which you pressed into a hole or depression in a plank of soft wood. Moving the bow back and forth causes the hard wood pencil to spin, and as you press down the friction between the pieces of wood makes the plank smoulder. Next you need tinder – dried rags, wood shavings, or grass – that will easily catch fire. The tinder is placed where the pieces of wood touch, and hopefully – with a bit of blowing and encouragement – the tinder will catch fire. Once you had fire, the aim was to keep it alight. Not surprisingly, the search was on for something more convenient.

In John Walker's time the tinder box was probably the most common fire-lighting device. Using the friction of a piece of iron or steel struck with a piece of flint, its great advantage over a fire drill is that it will instantly produce white-hot sparks. These are allowed to fall onto the tinder stored in the box, which with a bit of skill can be encouraged to smoulder and catch fire. The tinder box was fairly portable, but certainly wasn't quick enough to allow you to light a candle if you wanted to get up in the middle of the night. Actually getting the tinder to catch fire was tricky, but you also had to transfer the fire to a candle, and then to whatever you wanted to light. It is actually rather difficult to transfer the flame directly to wood. To circumvent the process, sulphur-tipped matches were sometimes used. These didn't themselves make fire, but the sulphur would catch from the tinder, and would in turn light the wooden match.

Chemistry was applied to making fire from the seventeenth century. In Germany in 1669, an alchemist called

John Walker's friction match.

Brand (rather a good name for a chap who made fire) discovered phosphorus by boiling urine. When exposed to air at anything like room temperature, it spontaneously catches fire. The difficulty lies in controlling it, and phosphorus burns are particularly nasty. Robert Boyle marketed a match based on sulphur-coated wooden matches being drawn through phosphorus-coated paper. It was very expensive, and didn't catch on. The Promethean match was an equally frightening invention, but at least the ingredients didn't spontaneously catch fire. It consisted of a glass vial of concentrated sulphuric acid (not something you'd want to carry around in your pocket) wrapped in paper, which also contained something to provide oxygen, and something like sugar to catch fire. Breaking the glass vial (said to have been done with the teeth) caused the whole lot to catch fire. The dawning of the steam age and the start of the industrial revolution happened without a safe, portable and convenient way of making fire.

So that was the state of play when John Walker of Stockton-on-Tees came along. He was born on 29 May 1781, the third son of John and Mary, at 104 High Street, Stockton, where his father ran a grocery, wine and spirit shop. John went to grammar school, where he learnt Latin and got a taste for science. He left school at fifteen to become apprentice to Stockton's principal surgeon, Watson Alcock. By the time he obtained his surgical qualifications in London and returned to become Alcock's assistant, he had become too squeamish to be a surgeon. So instead he went to Durham and then York to train as a chemist. Finally, in 1819, at the age of thirty-eight, he opened a chemist and druggist shop at 59 High Street, Stockton. (It is now Boots the Chemist, which seems fitting.) He was nicknamed 'Stockton's Encyclopaedia' because of his great knowledge of botany, geology, astronomy and, most importantly, chemistry.

We know a little about John Walker's chemist business from his day-book, in which he recorded his sales. These included medicines, though the frequent use of mercury compounds must have polished off a few customers. He also sold cosmetics, and ingredients for cooking – the sort of things you can find in a chemist's today. From about 1825 he recorded several sales of combustible mixtures to farmers and young men, possibly for making percussion caps for guns. He sold a variety of mixtures, and we don't know if this is because he was merely filling orders, or because he was

experimenting. On one occasion he had been preparing such a mixture when he accidentally scraped the mixing stick on the hearth – and it caught fire.

The crucial thing was not that the powder caught fire – he knew it would do that, and others made similar mixtures. The point, which he seems to have seen immediately, was that it was capable of setting the stick on fire. His mixture consisted of potassium chlorate and black antimony sulphide, which ignites at a very low temperature. Friction of the stick on the hearth raised the surface temperature just enough for the mixture to catch. Walker used the mixture to tip matches, and called them 'Sulphurata Hyper-oxygenata Frict.', a deliberately misleading name to protect the formula. The first sale, to a solicitor called Mr Hixon, is recorded in the day-book on 7 April 1827. He also wrote that this was 'box No. 30', which suggests he might have given the first twenty-nine away. Later that year, he renamed his invention: on 7 September 1827 he sold 'Friction Lights' to a Mr. Fenwick. Eighty-four Lights cost 10d, the tin 2d.

Walker seems to have decided not to let his good fortune change his life. Although urged to patent his matches by, among others, Michael Faraday, Walker declined. 'I doubt not it will be a benefit to the public,' he said. 'Let them have it. I shall always be able to obtain sufficient for myself.'

Stockton-on-Tees is heavy with memorials, from John Walker Square off the High Street (with a bust of the wrong John Walker!) and the Matchmaker Brasserie, and the John Walker pub round the corner, to original matches in the Green Dragon Museum, open Mon–Fri 9–5; 01642 674308. There are plaques at the location of his chemist's shop in the High Street (now Boots!) and opposite at his birthplace.

50. EDWIN BUDDING AND THE LAWNMOWER

A lawn is a patch of grass that is always cut short. Two hundred years ago lawns were rare, because cutting the grass was such hard work; at Blenheim Palace fifty labourers were employed full time looking after the pleasure gardens and the lawns. They used to cut the grass every ten days in summer, a line of scythesmen or 'mowers' starting early in the morning when the dew was on the grass, for the scythe worked better when the grass was wet. Even skilled scythesmen left swirls or sear marks on the grass, because the scythe was swung in a half-circle, and the blade was often serrated.

In Britain today, the majority of houses have some sort of lawn, and large houses may have acres. Public parks have huge lawns, and cricket pitches, golf courses, tennis courts and football fields have all become practical. The difference has been brought about mainly by the lawnmower, invented by Edwin Beard Budding of Stroud in Gloucestershire.

BUDDING'S
PATENT GRASS-CUTTING MACHINE.

Edwin Budding's lawnmower. 'Country gentlemen may find in using my machine themselves an amusing, useful and healthy exercise.'

Edwin Budding was born late in 1795, the illegitimate son of a farmer. He began to work for a carpenter, but moved into the iron foundries, and became a freelance engineer because he was good at solving engineering problems. Between 1825 and 1830 he developed a pistol that was allegedly better than Sam Colt's revolver of 1835. In 1843 he improved the carding machine, with the help of George Lister. He designed new types of spanner and lathe. But his great triumph was the mowing machine, which he invented in 1830. According to legend, he was working at the time in Brimscombe mill where a rotary cutter was used to trim the nap from woollen cloth. The idea came to him that a similar machine could be built to cut the nap off lawns. He went into partnership with John Ferrabee, whose job was to sort out the patent, the business and the marketing, and together they produced a 19-inch mower with a wrought-iron frame. One of the first machines went to the Regents Park Zoological Gardens, where the foreman Mr Curtis said, 'it does as much work as six or eight men with scythes and brooms . . . performing the whole so perfectly as not to leave a mark of any kind behind.'

The patent, no. 6081 of 1830, is clear and specific: the invention is 'a new combination and application of machinery for the purpose of cropping or shearing the vegetable surface of lawns', and the drawings show the precise construction. The main roller at the back provided drive via gears to the cutting cylinder, and there was a second roller in the middle for adjusting the height of the cut. The grass cuttings were thrown forward into a tray. Later versions were made with an additional handle in front to pull, with wider frames, and so on, but the basic design remains essentially unchanged to this day.

The patent also says: 'Country gentlemen may find in using my machine themselves an amusing, useful and healthy exercise.' In one sense that was the power of Budding's idea, for it enabled ordinary people to cut their own grass; they did not need to pay men with scythes. That's why so many people have lawns today.

By 1832 Ransomes of Ipswich were selling Budding machines. Their advertisements said: 'This machine is so easy to manage, that persons unpractised in the Art of Mowing, may cut the Grass on Lawns, Pleasure Grounds, and Bowling Greens with ease.' Meanwhile their instructions were rather simpler than those on many of today's gadgets: '. . . take hold of the handles, as in driving a barrow, . . . push the machine steadily forward along the greensward, without lifting the handles, but rather exerting a moderate pressure downwards . . .'.

More than a thousand were sold in the 1830s, but alas Mr Budding died of a stroke in 1846, so he probably didn't reap the full reward from his sharp idea. His partner John Ferrabee owned the Phoenix Iron Works in Thrupp, just outside Stroud, and that is where the first machines were made.

The Phoenix Mill has risen from the ashes and instead of mowing machines now produces wonderful books – including this one.

51. WILLIAM COOKWORTHY'S CHINA

Broadly speaking, there are three types of pottery – earthenware, as used in flowerpots; stoneware, as in casseroles; and porcelain, used for the finest teacups. The difference between earthenware and porcelain mugs or cups is obvious if you drink from them; the porcelain is smoother and finer and feels colder. Until the early eighteenth century the only porcelain available in Britain was imported from the Far East, and was therefore called china. Because it was clearly of better quality than the material most people had, there was some enthusiasm to crack the secrets of the mysterious east and make porcelain in Britain.

The man who did it was William Cookworthy, born in Kingsbridge in Devon on 12 April 1705, the eldest of seven children in a Quaker family. When he was thirteen his father died, and the next year William was apprenticed to a firm of chemists and druggists run by Silvanus Bevan in London. About 1733 he established a wholesale chemist's business in Plymouth. He married Sarah Berry – they eventually had five daughters – and he became a Minister for the Society of Friends, which meant that he travelled a good deal around Devon and Cornwall in order to preach.

He was always interested in geology, and he may have read a book about the manufacture of porcelain in China, even though the recipe was still secret. His brother had been to China, and may well have brought home first-hand accounts of the business. The critical clue came in 1745; Cookworthy describes in a letter of 5 May to a surgeon friend how he had recently met an American who discovered china clay – kaolin – in Virginia. Cookworthy reckoned that if it existed in Virginia it might well exist in Cornwall too; so he started searching in earnest, and in due course he found deposits of the right sort of minerals at Tregonnin Hill in the parish of Germo, near Helston. Then he found better and more accessible deposits at St Stephen near St Austell, on the property of Lord Camelford, who was interested, and helped with the development.

Cookworthy took samples back to Plymouth and there began his experiments. When he heated one sample to white heat in a crucible he obtained 'a beautiful semi-diaphanous white substance'. He soon discovered that all he needed was 'china stone' or petuntse which was quarried as a local building material and 'china clay' or kaolin, which was used to line the smelting furnaces. So much for the 'secret ingredients'!

Progress was slow, but in 1768 Cookworthy took out a patent for the manufacture of porcelain, and with Lord Camelford's help opened a factory at Coxside,

William Cookworthy a year before his death in 1779.

Plymouth, where he employed fifty or sixty people, including an experienced porcelain painter and enameller from Sèvres. However, the business was quickly in financial trouble; Cookworthy had difficulty maintaining a consistent product, and the cost of coal for firing the kiln was a serious problem. There was great demand for porcelainware, but unfortunately he could not make it profitably, so a few years later he sold his patent to his partner, Richard Champion of Bristol. At the same time they applied for an extension of the patent, but this was bitterly opposed by Josiah Wedgwood and other Staffordshire potters, who wanted to make porcelain themselves. Champion also ran into financial problems, and in 1777 sold the business on to a company in Staffordshire, where the coal was cheaper.

William Cookworthy was described as a tall, venerable man, with a three-cornered hat and bushy, curly wig, a mild but intellectual countenance, and full of conversation. He became well known in the scientific world; in August 1768 Captain James Cook, Sir Joseph Banks and Dr Solander dropped in to dine with him just before they set off around the world in their second-hand coal barge to observe the transit of Venus. Cookworthy died in 1780; the Bristol factory closed in 1781; and by 1858 there were forty-two companies producing 65,000 tonnes of china clay every year.

The Cookworthy Museum at 108 Fore Street in Kingsbridge, South Devon, has a small display of Cookworthy material; 01548 853235. Try also the Plymouth Museum; 01752 668000.

52. COLIN PULLINGER AND HIS PERPETUAL MOUSETRAP

Mice have always plagued people; ever since the first cave-dwellers began to store food in a larder, mice have been there to make the most of it. Whenever people move into any sort of home, mice move in right alongside; for thousands of years people must have been inventing ways to get rid of them. So the mousetrap has become a sort of symbol of human ingenuity – and this is just what *Local Heroes* is all about.

The earliest mousetraps were probably just holes in the ground; the advanced versions were bottles sunk into the ground, so that the mice could not climb out up the slippery walls.

Among the earliest known mechanical traps was the pit-fall trap, which was essentially a hole in the ground with a trapdoor, traditionally baited with a mixture of oatmeal and honey. The mouse

Figure of man playing a pipe modelled by Jacques Thibault and produced by Cookworthy at the Plymouth factory.

Colin Pullinger's perpetual mousetrap. He claimed that in a single trap he caught twenty-eight mice in one night!

came along, smelled the bait, stepped on the trapdoor, and dropped into the pit – or probably into a bucket of water.

Today the traditional bait is cheese; indeed poor-quality or plain cheap Cheddar cheeses are sometimes called 'mousetrap'. Most modern traps have metal springs; when the mouse touches the bait it releases a catch and a stiff wire loop snaps viciously down on the mouse's neck, usually killing it instantly. These traps are neat and powerful, but they have two disadvantages. First they are considered by some to be inhumane; occasionally the mouse is not killed, but injured and left in pain. Secondly, the trap can catch only one mouse at a time. Once it's sprung it's sprung, and other mice can come along and eat the cheese with impunity.

Both of these drawbacks were solved by Colin Pullinger, a Hampshire man, born in 1814 in Ivy Cottage in Selsey. Despite all the claims on his trade card, he eventually inherited his father's house and carpentry business, and then, about 1860, he invented a new mousetrap. This was a 'perpetual mousetrap' – one that would catch mouse after mouse – and the mice were not killed or even injured.

The trap had a hole in the middle of the top, for the mice to go in, attracted by the smell of the bait kept in a perforated bait-box inside. Below the entrance hole was the critical mechanism, a cruciform beam like a see-saw which the mouse would tip with its weight. Once the see-saw had tipped, the mouse could no longer reach the entrance hole; so its only way out of the small compartment was through a one-way door into the end of the box. Once it had gone through this door, there was no escape, and the trap was set ready for the next mouse, which would find its way to the other end of the box. Colin always stressed how humane it was; the mice were unharmed, and could presumably be set free in your neighbour's garden!

Colin Pullinger's mousetrap was incredibly successful, both operationally and financially. He claimed in his advertising that he had once caught twenty-

COLIN PULLINGER,
SELSEY, NEAR CHICHESTER,
Contractor, Inventor, Fisherman, and Mechanic,

FOLLOWING THE VARIOUS TRADES OF A

BUILDER, CARPENTER, JOINER, SAWYER, UNDERTAKER

Tanner, Cooper, Painter, Glazier, Wooden Pump Maker,

PAPER HANGER, BELL HANGER, SIGN PAINTER,
BOAT BUILDER,

CLOCK CLEANER, REPAIRER OF LOCKS, AND KEYS FITTED,

Repairer of Umbrellas and Parasols, Mender of China and Glass,

Copying Clerk, Letter Writer, Accountant, Teacher of Navigation,

GROCER, BAKER, FARMER,

Assessor and Collector of Taxes, Surveyor, House Agent, Engineer, Land

Measurer, Assistant Overseer, Clerk at the Parish Vestry Meetings,

Clerk to the Selsey Police, Clerk to the Selsey Sparrow Club,

Has served at Sea in the four Quarters of the World, as Seaman, Cook,

Steward, Mate and Navigator.

THE MAKER AND INVENTOR OF THE FOLLOWING:

AN IMPROVED HORSE HOE, AN IMPROVED SCARIFIER,

A newly-invented Couch Grass Rake, a Machine to Tar Ropes, Model of a

Vessel to cut asunder Chains put across the Mouth of a Harbour,

A CURIOUS MOUSE TRAP,

Made on a scientific principle, where each one caught resets the trap to catch its next

neighbour, requires no fresh baiting, and will catch them by dozens,

A Rat Trap on a peculiar Construction,

That will catch and put them into the Trap,

An improved Mole Trap, an improved Velocipede, Model of a fast-sailing

Yacht on an improved construction, 2ft long, and challenged to sail

against any boat of the same length in the world, &c, &c, &c.

CRABS, LOBSTERS, AND PRAWNS SENT TO ANY PART OF ENGLAND,

MOUSE TRAPS LET ON HIRE.

Colin Pullinger's trade card.

eight mice in one trap in a single night, and that in nine months a farmer had caught nearly a thousand mice in one trap.

The factory grew until Pullinger employed forty men and boys; he was the biggest employer in Selsey. They had horse-powered circular saws and drills; they could make a trap in four and a half minutes, and they made 960 a week. By 1885 they had sold two million, at half a crown apiece, and mousetraps went on being made in Selsey until 1920.

The success of Colin Pullinger's enterprise lends support to the aphorism coined by the American writer Ralph Waldo Emerson: 'If a man write a better book, preach a better sermon, or make a better mousetrap than his neighbour, tho' he build his house in the woods, the world will make a beaten path to his door.'

Colin Pullinger's house, Ivy Cottage, still stands in Selsey, but there is no obvious trace of the yard where he made his mousetraps.

53. LIBORIO PEDRAZZOLLI AND HIS SWIMMING UMBRELLAS

People have always wanted to be able to flash through the water with more speed and more freedom; hence the attraction of flippers, snorkels and other swimming aids. Among the more splendid inventions in this area were the swimming umbrellas dreamed up by Liborio Pedrazzolli.

Mr Pedrazzolli came over to England from Italy in about 1880, married an English girl, and set himself up in business as a wholesale and export looking-glass manufacturer at 11 Hoxton Street in north-east London. He must have reflected carefully about improving the efficiency of his swimming, and reasoned that he got a good push on the water when he kicked with his feet, but his hands seemed to slip through almost without pulling him forwards. So in 1896 he applied for a patent for mini-umbrellas to hold in his hands and increase their grip on the water. His patent describes how they work: 'When the forward stroke takes place in swimming the apparati close up and thereby offer a minimum amount of resistance to the water, but when the return stroke is made the apparati expand in umbrella form, and the resistance thus offered enables the swimmer to pull or propel himself through the water at a speed hitherto impossible.'

There was only one way to test them; I made some myself. The result was interesting, although not conclusive. They certainly did give a good grip on the water, but only after about 12–13 inches of the stroke, because they were quite slow to open. Meanwhile they slightly impeded all hand movements, so my hands tired more quickly. After practising for half an hour I decided I would be better off without them – but perhaps if they had been lighter in construction, and a little longer, and I had persevered, I too might have been able to swim at a speed hitherto impossible!

What were Pedrazzolli's premises in Hoxton Street have become a school.

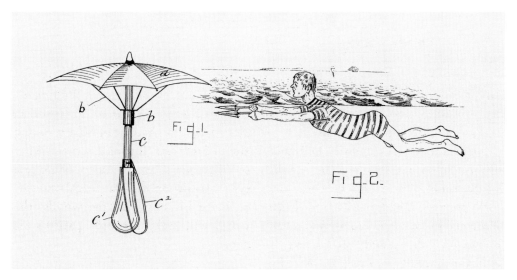

Liborio Pedrazzolli's patent swimming umbrellas: 'when the return stroke is made the apparati expand in umbrella form, and the resistance thus offered enables the swimmer to pull or propel himself through the water at a speed hitherto impossible'.

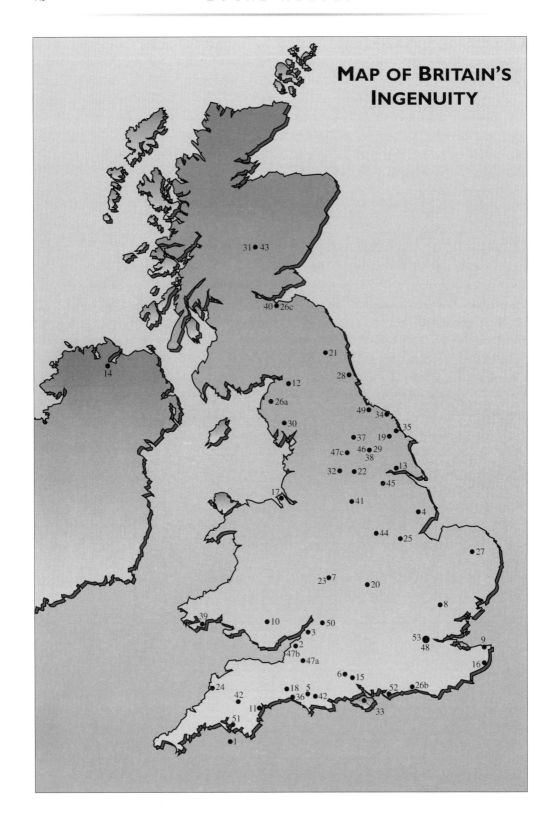

MAP OF BRITAIN'S
INGENUITY

31● 43

40●26c

21

14   12

28

26a

30   49 34

35

37 19

47c●46●29

38

32 22

13

45

17

41

4

44 25

27

23●7

20

8

39

10   50

3

53

2   48

47b●47a   9

6 15   16

24   42   18 5   52 26b

36 42

11   33

51

1

Key:

1. Henry Winstanley
2. Humphry Davy
3. Edward Jenner
4. William Marwood
5. Henry Moule
6. Florence Nightingale
7. William Withering
8. William Harvey
9. Hertha Ayrton
10. Richard Trevithick
11. Isambard Kingdom Brunel
12. Thomas Edmondson
13. Ted Wright
14. William Coppin
15. Edward Lyon Berthon
16. Henry Bessemer
17. George William Garrett
18. John Stringfellow
19. Sir George Cayley
20. Dennis Gabor
21. David Brewster
22. John Clayton
23. William Murdoch
24. Goldsworthy Gurney
25. Isaac Newton
26a. John Dalton
26b. Thomas Young
26c. James Maxwell
27. William Hyde Wollaston
28. Joseph Wilson Swan
29. Tempest Anderson
30. John Mackereth
31. Nevil Maskelyne
32. John Michell
33. John 'Earthquake' Milne
34. William Scoresby
35. William Smith
36. Mary Anning
37. William Buckland
38. Alcuin
39. Robert Recorde
40. John Napier
41. Nicholas Saunderson
42. George Parker Bidder
43. Charles Hutton
44. George Green
45. George Boole
46. Moses Bruine Cotsworth
47a. William Oliver
47b. Sarah Guppy
47c. Thomas Gaddes
48. Christopher Pinchbeck
49. John Walker
50. Edwin Budding
51. William Cookworthy
52. Colin Pullinger
53. Liborio Pedrazzolli

CHRONOLOGY

LOCAL HEROES	HISTORIC EVENTS	
c. 800 Alcuin's *Propositiones ad Acuendos Juvenes*	Charlemagne crowned Holy Roman Emperor Christmas Day	800
	Mary Tudor (crowned)	1553
1557 Robert Recorde invents equals sign		
	Elizabeth I	1558
	William Shakespeare born	1564
	James I	1603
	Gunpowder plot	1605
1610 Galileo observes moons of Jupiter		
	Authorised Version of the Bible	1611
	Witches of Pendle tried	1612
1614 John Napier's book of logarithms		
	Pilgrim Fathers set sail	1620
	Charles I	1625
1628 Wm Harvey's book on circulation		
1642 Galileo dies		
1642 Isaac Newton born		
	English civil war	1642
	Taj Mahal completed	1652
	Charles II	1660
	Royal Society founded	1660
	Great Plague	1665
1666 Isaac Newton's *annus mirabilis*	Great Fire of London	1666
1672 Isaac Newton's letter on the spectrum		
	Wren's Greenwich Observatory	1675
	James II	1685
1687 John Clayton Rector at Crofton		
1687 Isaac Newton's *Principia*		
	William III and Mary II	1688
	Bank of England founded	1691
1698 T. Savery's patent for 'raiseing water'		
1698 H. Winstanley's Eddystone Lighthouse		
	Anne	1702

1703	Eddystone Lighthouse destroyed
1711	N. Saunderson Lucasian Professor
1712	First Newcomen engine, Dudley

Last witch executed in England	1712
George I	1714
Fahrenheit's temperature scale	1714
Walpole first Prime Minister	1721
George II	1727
UK adopts Gregorian calendar	1752

1754	Joseph Black's thesis published
1757	John Gough, blind philosopher, born
1759	John Smeaton's Eddystone Lighthouse

George III	1760
Lunar Society of Birmingham	1766

1762	Matthew Boulton's Soho Manufactory
1768	Pinchbeck's 'nocturnal remembrancer'
1768	Wm Cookworthy's porcelain patent
1769	J. Cook and J. Banks sail to Tahiti
1769	James Watt's first steam engine patent
1771	Joseph Priestley makes oxygen
1771	Richard Arkwright's cotton mill
1774	Maskelyne measures mass of Earth
1775	William Withering discovers *Digitalis*
1775	Charles Hutton invents contour lines
1775	First WC patent: Alexander Cumming
1778	Joseph Bramah's water-closet patent
1779	James Watt's copying machine
1782	William Watts makes lead shot
1783	John Michell describes a black hole
1784	W. Murdoch's model steam locomotive
1787	John Dalton sees aurora
1788	Edward Jenner writes about cuckoos
1788	G. White's *Natural History of Selborne*

Transit of Venus observed	1769
Boulton & Watt partnership	1774
American War of Independence	1775
James Cook discovers Hawaii	1778
Montgolfiers' hot-air balloon	1782
French revolution	1789

1790	Joseph Bramah's unpickable lock
1791	John Barber patents gas turbine

Metric system in France	1795

1796	Edward Jenner vaccinates J. Phipps
1796	Geo. Cayley's whirling-arm machine
1797	Joseph Bramah's beer engine
1798	H. Cavendish measures mass of Earth
1798	Humphry Davy tries laughing gas

Malthus's Essay on population	1798

1799	'The flower of physic is Withering'	Rosetta Stone found in Egypt 1799
1799	J. Black dies without spilling milk	
1800	W.H. Wollaston's camera lucida	
1801	Richard Trevithick's steam carriage	
1802	William Murdoch lights Soho with gas	
1803	J. Dalton introduces atomic weights	
1804	R. Trevithick's Penydaren locomotive	
1806	George Parker Bidder born Dartmoor	
1811	Mary Anning finds ichthyosaurus	
1812	Sarah Guppy's improved tea urn	
1814	T. Young deciphers Rosetta Stone	
1815	W. Smith's geological map of Britain	Battle of Waterloo 1815
1816	David Brewster's kaleidoscope	
1820	Sewage pollution of Windermere	**George IV** 1820
1820	Florence Nightingale born in Florence	
1821	William Buckland finds hyena bones	
1823	Mary Anning finds first plesiosaur	
1824	Joe Aspdin patents Portland Cement	
1825	Goldsworthy Gurney's steam carriage	
1826	David Douglas sends Douglas Fir	
1828	George Green's mathematical essay	
1828	Mary Anning finds first pterodactyl	
1830	Edwin Budding's lawnmower	**William IV** 1830
1831	Fitzroy and Darwin sail in *Beagle*	BAAS founded 1831
1831	Sarah Guppy's ingenious bedstead	
1833	G. Boole's vision in a field in Doncaster	
1833	T.R. Robinson's cup anemometer	
1834	Ed. Lyon Berthon's screw propeller	
1837	Thomas Edmondson's rail ticket	**Victoria** 1837
1839	Goldsworthy Gurney's Bude Light	Penny post in England 1839
1840	W. Whewell invents the word 'scientist'	Indian mutiny 1840
1841	J. Whitworth's universal screw threads	Brunel's GWR reaches Bristol 1841
1842	Wm Coppin launches *Great Northern*	
1845	G.P. Bidder's railway swing bridge	
1846	C.P. Smyth Astron. Royal for Scotland	
1847	Brunel's atmospheric railway	
1847	J. Joule's mechanical equivalent of heat	
1848	J. Stringfellow achieves powered flight	
		Cholera kills 55,000 in Britain 1849
		Great Exhibition, London 1851
1853	Geo. Cayley's New Flyer carries man	
1854	Florence Nightingale sails for Crimea	

'Great stink' in Parliament   1858

1859 Darwin's *Origin of species*
1860 Henry Moule patents earth-closet
1860 C. Pullinger's perpetual mouse-trap
1861 Thomas Crapper sets up as plumber
1862 Alexander Parkes produces parkesine
1863 James Clerk Maxwell's colour photo

London Underground   1863
Pasteurisation   1864
Mendel's Law of Heredity   1865
Great Eastern lays Atlantic cable 1866

1866 John Getty McGee's Ulster overcoat
1875 William Marwood hangs first victim
1875 Henry Hunnings's carbon microphone

Alexander Graham Bell's
telephone   1875

1875 SS *Bessemer*'s maiden and last voyage
1877 John Jeyes patents Jeyes Fluid
1879 Geo. Wm Garrett launches *Resurgam*
1889 John Boyd Dunlop's pneumatic tyres

Diesel engine   1892
1893 Mikael Pedersen's tension bikes   Henry Ford makes first car   1893
X-rays discovered by Röntgen 1895
1896 Fred Lanchester's petrol-driven car   Nobel Prizes founded   1896
1896 L. Pedrazzolli's swimming umbrellas   1st modern Olympic Games   1896
1897 Dr T. Gaddes's automatic egg-boiler
1900 John Milne's seismology laboratory   Quantum theory, Max Planck   1900
Edward VII   1901

1902 T. Anderson snaps Mt Pelée eruption
1904 H. Ayrton's paper to Royal Society

Einstein's special relativity 1905
George V   1910

1932 G. Malloch's combined salmon gaff etc.

Edward VIII, George VI   1936

1937 Ted Wright finds first Ferriby boat
1946 H. Ferguson's TE20 – the 'wee Fergie'
1947 Dennis Gabor's imaginary hologram
1948 Nicholas Kove's first Airfix Kit

Elizabeth II   1952

1958 J. Mackereth's pneumatic bottom corer

FURTHER READING

When researching our heroes we look at many books, booklets, and articles, some of which are tucked away in obscure places. Here is a selection of material that is relatively easy to find. By far the best single source of information is the *Dictionary of National Biography*, published by the Oxford University Press. Most of the heroes appear there.

GENERAL BOOKS

Brown, G.I., *The Guinness History of Inventions*, Guinness, 1996
Clarke, Donald (ed.), *The Encyclopedia of Inventions*, Marshall Cavendish, 1977
Garvin, Wilbert and O'Rawe, Des, *Northern Ireland Scientists and Inventors*, Blackstaff/Queen's University, 1993
Harris, Melvin, *ITN Book of Firsts*, Michael O'Mara Books, 1994
Robertson, Patrick, *The Shell Book of Firsts*, Ebury Press, 1974
Rolt, L.T.C., *Great Engineers*, Bell, 1962

BOOKS ABOUT PARTICULAR HEROES

Beaver, Patrick, *The Match Makers*, Henry Melland, 1985
Bessemer, Sir Henry, *An Autobiography*, Engineering, 1905
Clarke, E.F., *George Parker Bidder, the Calculating Boy*, KSL Publications, 1983
Fisher, Richard B., *Edward Jenner*, Andre Deutsch, 1991
Hammond, John H. and Austin, Jill, *The Camera Lucida in Art and Science*, Adam Hilger, 1987
McHale, Des, *George Boole, his Life and Work*, Boole Press, 1985
Majdalaney, Fred, *The Red Rocks of Eddystone* [Winstanley], Longman, 1959; White Lion, 1974
Penderill-Church, John, *William Cookworthy*, Bradford Barton, 1972
Penrose, Harald, *An Ancient Air* [Stringfellow], Airlife, 1988
Rolt, L.T.C., *Isambard Kingdom Brunel*, Longman, 1957; Penguin, 1980
——, *The Cornish Giant* [Trevithick], Lutterworth, 1960
Sharpe, Evelyn, *Hertha Ayrton, A Memoir*, Edward Arnold & Co., 1926
Tickell, Sir Crispin, *Mary Anning of Lyme Regis*, Lyme Regis Philpot Museum, 1996
Wright, Edward, *The Ferriby Boats, Seacraft of the Bronze Age*, Routledge, 1990

INDEX